ENDORSI

Most believers know the importance of our words but still say the opposite of God's Word! And most wonder why their life, destiny and prayers seem sabotaged. After reading this book, you will supernaturally speak right words and enter heaven on earth.

SID ROTH
Host, *It's Supernatural!*

If there is one thing that I am absolutely certain of, it is the biblical truth that life and death are in the power of the tongue. Our words can release blessings or curses; life or death. In this thought-provoking, yet practical work, *The Prophetic and Healing Power of Your Words*, Becky Dvorak takes you on a journey of insight, revelation, and impartation of a fresh conviction in the area of the words you speak. This book will empower you to "speak life" and see the supernatural power of God manifested in your life as you learn to consistently declare God's Word. Healing, deliverance, victory, and blessing are in your mouth, and now is the time to release them.

DR. KYNAN BRIDGES
Bestselling author, *90 Days of Power Prayer*
Senior Pastor, Grace & Peace Global Fellowship

Becky Dvorak has operated in the prophetic and healing ministry for many years. Her healing ministry has brought miracles and freedom to Christians around the world, and her work among children in Guatemala is a model for meeting the physical and spiritual needs of children and adults. As a frequent contributing writer to *SpiritLed Woman*, Becky has encouraged and equipped women throughout the church for the ministry of prophetic healing. This book includes her wisdom and experience with years of life-changing prophetic healing ministry.

LEILANI HAYWOOD
Former Editor of *SpiritLed Woman/Charisma*

In *The Prophetic and Healing Power of Your Words*, Becky Dvorak brings great clarity and practical implementation to guide you in equipping and empowering your tongue. Deeply influenced in her life and ministry by the writings of Lester Sumrall and Smith Wigglesworth, Becky relays through this book, a deep understanding of the Word as well as stories of powerful application and testimony. If you have a growing desire to grasp and unleash the God-given power of your words, you will enjoy this book as an activator for your faith!

WILMER and REBECCA SINGLETON
Founders of 1Voice Global

—THE—
Prophetic & Healing
POWER OF YOUR
WORDS

OTHER DESTINY IMAGE BOOKS BY BECKY DVORAK

Dare to Believe

Greater than Magic

The Healing Creed

THE
Prophetic & Healing
POWER OF YOUR
WORDS

Creating an Atmosphere
for the Miraculous

BECKY DVORAK

DESTINY IMAGE® PUBLISHERS, INC.

PO Box 310, Shippensburg, PA 17257-0310

"Promoting Inspired Lives"

This book and all other Destiny Image and Destiny Image Fiction books available at Christian bookstores and distributors worldwide.

Cover design by Eileen Rockwell

Page design by Terry Clifton

For more information on foreign distributors, call 717-532-3040.

Or reach us on the Internet: www.destinyimage.com

ISBN 13 TP: 978-0-7684-4329-5

ISBN 13 Ebook: 978-0-7684-4330-1

ISBN 13 LP: 978-0-7684-4331-8

ISBN 13 HC: 978-0-7684-4332-5

For Worldwide Distribution, Printed in the U.S.A.

1 2 3 4 5 6 / 21 20 19 18

DEDICATION

I dedicate this work, *The Prophetic & Healing Power of Your Words,* to all who are ready to tap into the prophetic vocabulary of the Holy Spirit and activate life, strength, and healing into your very being, and unleash the power of the Spirit with your words to a lost and dying world that so desperately needs healing of the spirit, soul, and body in these last days.

ACKNOWLEDGMENTS

I would like to sincerely thank Destiny Image Publishers for the fine job they have done to help deliver this message, *The Prophetic & Healing Power of Your Words,* to you. Special thanks to Larry Sparks (publisher), Angela R. Shears (editor), Eileen Rockwell (cover designer) Terry Clifton (page designer), John Martin (production manager). I'm blessed and honored to work with you.

CONFESSION OF FAITH TO WIELD THE TONGUE

I wield the power of my tongue to heal and protect my faith in God so that it is not rendered useless (James 1:26), emulate Yeshua, the Living Word, and release prophetic healing by the power of my spoken words.

I bridle my tongue (James 1:26), to keep my soul from trouble (Proverbs 21:23). I will not speak of wickedness, or utter deceit (Job 27:4). I extinguish the fiery flames of hell (James 3:4-6), as I repent of a murderous tongue, and will no longer listen to or speak gossip (Romans 1:28-32; Proverbs 26:20), but will speak the truth in love (Ephesians 4:15).

I will not defile my body with negative speech and faithless words (Matthew 15:11), but will study God's promises to know how to give faith-filled answers (Proverbs 15:28), utilize the power of pleasant words that are sweet to the soul and healing to the bones (Proverbs 16:24), I will meditate upon the Scriptures day and night (Joshua 1:8), so that I will prosper in all things and be in health (3 John 1:2).

My speech is seasoned with salty grace (Colossians 4:6), His goodness that edifies (Ephesians 4:29), wholesomeness, like a tree of life (Proverbs 15:4), it brings forth wisdom (Proverbs 10:31), and spurs others to believe for their healing while it is still today (Hebrews 3:13).

Like Elohim, I create by words of faith (Genesis 1:1-4), I utilize the creative force of my tongue and give life to the dead and call into being that which does not exist (Romans 4:17).

With my voice I exalt the name that is above all names, Yeshua, Jesus, the King of kings, and the Lord of lords, and not the sickness or disease (Philippians 2:9-11). I openly give thanks because He is good, and His mercy endures forever (Psalm 118:1).

CONTENTS

INTRODUCTION

Daily I receive prayer requests and messages filled with heart-felt pleas from God's people begging to be taught how to heal their bodies. And every day the confessions are mounting that they just don't know how to speak the healing word over themselves. They are unlearned in the prophetic power of their words and desperate to be shown the way to healing and life.

One of the key objectives of this work is to empower your words to create atmospheres that release supernatural healing to your entire being—spirit, soul (mind and emotions), and into the physical body.

PART ONE

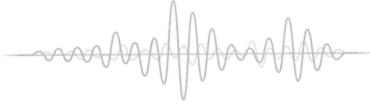

THE FOUNDATIONAL
POWER OF WORDS

CHAPTER 1

EMULATE THE LIVING WORD

Have you ever wondered how the prophetic realm works? Recently, I was privy to the secret workings of just how this happens. Read the following and gain wisdom from this prophetic encounter.

A visiting pastor at a healing seminar where I ministered in Ocala, Florida, came to me after the teaching session and asked me, "Do you know you have an angel with you?" I told him, "Yes, I know I do and people often see him." This pastor and seer went on to explain what he saw.

He said, "Everywhere you go, he is right behind you. And he carries a book in his hands. While he stands right behind you, he opens this book and reads from its pages. You then repeat what he reads to you." He continues to tell me what he sees, then asks me, "Do you know what he does when you pause for a moment?" I reply, "Tell me, what he does." He says, "He quickly flips through his book and searches for something. And when he finds his next point, he reads it aloud to you, you hear him, and repeat what he narrates to you."

I explain to this man of God that many years ago I surrendered my voice to the Holy Spirit. And in addition to this, I can clearly remember the day, the afternoon in 1980, when I read through the New Testament and read in Matthew 10:19, *"Do not worry about how or what you should speak. For it will be given to you in that hour what you should speak."* And I knew

5

the voice of the Lord was speaking to me, revealing a time that I had not yet walked, but was to come, and this time is now.

It's now another meeting, another time, and in another place. I am about to stand and deliver the message from the Lord when I see an angel with a very powerful and shiny sword and he walks and stands where I am to stand. With both hands, he lifts the large and heavy sword of the Spirit above his head and thrusts it into the middle of the pulpit and stands his ground.

Many of God's ministers no longer preach or teach the Word, but we must. We are ministers of the Gospel of Jesus Christ, and His words are alive and well. And it is this living word that pierces the hearts of the people. It divides light from darkness. It exposes evil and convicts people, leading them to repentance and right standing with God.

Clever messages cannot redeem them. It cannot save their souls. In and of itself, a message from the pulpit is not meant to redeem. But ministers are created to declare the Word of the Lord with power, and signs and wonders following.

No matter who you are or where God has placed you in the Body of Christ, remember your purpose on this earth is to be about your heavenly Father's business. Work your heart to humbleness, surrender your voice. Allow the Spirit of God to play on the strings of your vocal chords a sweet melody that is well pleasing to the Father, one that woos people into the presence of an eternal relationship with Jehovah God. Use the prophetic and healing power of your words to redeem humankind with complete miracle-working manifestation.

I don't know about you, but I'm ready to enter into the promised land together, not just a few straggling into the boundaries of God's promises, but all of us together.

Word of the Lord

THE WORD OF THE LORD WOULD SAY TO YOU, *"Tap into the flow of the healing power of the supernatural. Turn on the spigot of the Spirit and drink freely of the Living Water and hydrate the dryness of your soul. Prophesy to your bones, speak life to the dead, recreate worn out body parts, and activate strength and healing through the power of your tongue."*

The Prophetic and Healing Power of Your Words

I stand in awe many times over as I witness the prophetic healing power of the Spirit change and rearrange the lives of God's people forever. A simple command of faith, "In Jesus' name, I command this cancerous tumor to shrivel up and die," and by morning the large tumor is gone and a woman's life is dramatically altered. In another meeting, I hear the Holy Spirit whisper in my ear, *"Call the people suffering from arthritis to come forward."* I do as He instructs, and about one hundred people step forward to the altar. I ask them to hold hands in groups as I lay my hand on one person in each group and release the prophetic healing power with my words, "I renounce arthritis and the demons behind this work." I lead them in a general prayer of repentance, and I touch them and simply speak forth, "Be healed in Jesus' name" and one by one they are delivered and healed.

Two women are standing in the healing line with the same problem, they are unable to produce natural tears. To save time, I stand between the two and stretch forth my hands and touch them both on their shoulders, I verbally release healing with the power of my spoken words, "In Jesus' name, I declare your eyes produce natural tears." And immediately both sets of eyes are healed and from the top to the bottom, the eyes are moistened and tears form.

An elderly woman can barely stand in the healing line as both hip joints are worn down and surgery is already scheduled later that week. I lightly touch her hip joints and I vocally create new ones and tell them, "Now, you function perfectly normal in the name of our Lord Jesus." I look her in the eye and tell her to move, bend over and touch her toes, walk and her hip joints are instantly recreated, healed, and all pain is gone as she effortlessly does what I tell her to do.

Prophetic healing is real, and it is for today.

But the enemy is afraid of the effectiveness of the prophetic healing and speaks lies among the Body of Christ. Some of our brothers and sisters in Christ believe prophetic healers are of the devil and these are occult practices. But I ask you to be reasonable, "Would satan desire for you to be delivered from demons? Would he want you to be healed from cancer and win people to Jesus with the words of your healing testimony? Would he be glad if your next door neighbor regained their sight? Or that your grandfather's deaf ears open so he can hear the Word of God preached again?"

For many years, and still counting, the devil agitates and stirs up the religious spirits among believers and hinders the mighty move of prophetic healing in all areas of life; spiritual, emotional, mental, and physical healing. But even though he may have been able to pull the wool over the eyes of a vast number of Christians for quite some time now, the Spirit of God is on the move, the remnant is on the rise, and the prophetic power of healing is on her tongue. It's time to join the ranks of God's remnant and take hold of the Kingdom of God by force, be about your heavenly Father's business, and win the lost in great numbers. Prophetic healing easily wins souls over to God.

Take the Kingdom of God by Force

Truly I tell you, among those born of women there has not risen anyone greater than John the Baptist; yet whoever is least in the kingdom of heaven is greater than he. From the days of John the Baptist until now, the kingdom of heaven has been subjected to violence, and violent people have been raiding it. For all the Prophets and the Law prophesied until John (Matthew 11:11-13 NIV).

The Law and the Prophets were proclaimed until John. Since that time, the good news of the kingdom of God is being preached, and everyone is forcing their way into it (Luke 16:16 NIV).

What is being said here to us in these two Scripture passages is that we have a decision to make, entering into the Kingdom of God is not easy. There is an evil force that works against us and tries to prevent us from entering into the promises of God. But God's people need to be equally forceful in this battle and activate our faith, and even fight the enemy with our supernatural weapons of faith.

With our son's amazing healing testimony—that I share with you in detail in *DARE to Believe,* chapter 11, pages 175-193—we had to take Marcos' healing by force. The spirit of death was not willing to let go of him. But we activated every weapon of faith given to us, and we raised him from the dead and recreated all his vital organs by prophetic healing power because they too were dead. We had to violently fight the devil head-on; and because we did not back down, we won. And he is alive and well.

Word of the Lord

THE SPIRIT OF THE LORD WOULD SAY TO YOU AGAIN, *"I have heard your longing to move in this gift of healing, and it is for you too. You take this message that I bring before you, devour it, and let your words produce for My glory in these last days."*

He Will Not Die, But Live

This is what can happen if you will align yourself with the prophetic and healing power of your words. A new boy in the last stage of HIV/AIDS arrived to our children's home that our ministry established and operates in Guatemala. We were required to redo all of the tests that had been done in the past, because the old paperwork was not sent with him. We were just told the young boy was going to die within two weeks. My husband and I said, "No! He will not die, but live." But when people don't believe in Jesus as the Healer, they lack hope for a miracle and life, and so for them there is only one outcome—death. While Christians have covenant rights with the Father to walk out of the Valley of the Shadow of Death by the redemptive blood of our Lord, Jesus Christ. And our first step of action to take is with the power of our faith-filled words.

We were required to bring him in for tests, and one was for *Tuberculosis* in the lungs. In the natural he had all the symptoms, but in the supernatural realm with God, our words supersede the natural and break forth into God's habitat where miracles abound. And this is what we needed. But we would have to contend with satan to make him move out of the way.

While they were prepping this young boy to take a sample from his lungs, the medical staff asked me who I was. And what was my relationship with this young boy. During conversation with the doctor I told him I believed in miracles and have witnessed such in that past and was standing in faith for this boy's healing. This doctor was clearly an unbeliever, and actually started to challenge my faith in a mocking manner. I stood my ground and did not back down from my stance.

I was then asked to step out of the room while they retrieved the sample necessary from his lungs. When the doctor came out he showed me the sample in the bottle and said, "This is classic TB." I replied, "In Jesus' name, no, he doesn't have it." The doctor did not back down from his stance either. He held up the sample and replied, "TB!" I said, "No, in Jesus' name." As he walked out of the room, he again pointed to the bottle and said sternly, "TB!" I responded, not rudely, but firmly and said, "No, he doesn't have it, in Jesus' name."

Your enemy, satan will fight you to the death if you allow him. But you must not let him have his way with you. Don't give him the satisfaction of having the last word. You hold true to your confession no matter what the situation looks like. You overcome with the word of your testimony. When he harasses you with words of death, you firmly respond to him, "No, I will not die, but live and glorify my Father in Heaven."

The boy had numerous tests that day, and we would receive all the results within a few weeks. First of all, the *Tuberculosis* test came back negative—even though he had all the symptoms of disease and the sample appeared to be classic TB. But, by spoken words of faith in the work of Christ, we brought this disease to its knees and it surrendered to the healing power of Yeshua. And that's not all, they could not find HIV in his body either.

Word of the Lord

THE SPIRIT OF THE LORD WOULD ENCOURAGE YOU THIS DAY, *"I am the bridge between mediocre Christianity and a lifestyle in the Spirit where dreams come true and visions are seen with the physical eye. Cross over this bridge with Me. Don't be afraid, I will lead you and guide you into all truth in My ways. And those of you who will follow Me will catapult into a higher realm where you and those around you will heal by the prophetic power of your words."*

Struggling with this Doctrinal Position that Words have Power?

Perhaps you struggle with this doctrinal position that your words have prophetic power to heal the sick, including yourself. If so, you're not alone, this is my beginning.

Back in the 1970s before I became a born-again Christian, I had never heard of such teaching. Back when I was a teenager, I would occasionally watch the American televangelist, Robert Schuller with my mom. If you recognize the name, you know his message was about the positive power of our words. I was drawn to the brightness of his message, but even then, this feel-good message did not reel me into the Kingdom of God. But it did instill within me hope, and that is the precursor to faith. And it certainly was not what I was accustomed to hearing from the pulpit.

And this is the heart of the problem, there is little teaching from the pulpit to equip God's people in the prophetic power of their words. To teach them to release words of victory in every situation. It's not comfortable for the man or woman of God to teach a message from the pulpit that convicts people to change. After all, people may bring up questions that church leaders are not able to or ready to answer because they personally have not been walking it out for themselves. Or church members may get upset that the pastor is questioning the way they speak or the way they act. Worse yet, they may pack up and move to the gathering down the road.

This passiveness from the pulpit hurts the Body of Christ. Many times lay people speak such negative words over themselves and suffer for their poor choice of words. Ministers, I am reminded of a song from Bob Dylan from 1979, "Gotta Serve Somebody." As people in the fivefold ministry, we have to understand that we have to decide whom we are going to serve. In the ministry we often confuse our purpose—we are to glorify God, not ourselves. And even though we are servants of the Most High, the people receive the benefits of our service; but our service is onto the Lord, not people, and certainly not the spirit of mammon and what it brings to the offering plate, that's service onto the devil himself.

If you have been following my writings, you know that I became born-again and baptized with the Holy Spirit in May 1979 when I was 18 years of age at Jesus People Church, downtown Minneapolis, on Hennepin Avenue in Minnesota. It was here that I first heard the voice of the Word and the Spirit of God. Even though I was spiritually dead and could not fully understand what was being taught, my spirit was being opened up to truth and God's Spirit was wooing me to enter into His Kingdom. And the moment I surrendered my life to Jesus, my spiritual ears were opened and I could comprehend the Word of God, and I also could readily discern and hear God's voice speaking to me.

Then due to a moral crisis, the church dispersed; but even still, many ministries were birthed out of that movement. And it was from there that my husband and I found ourselves in a little A-frame church called The Church of the Jubilee, under Roger and Marlene Davis. It was here, in the

1980s, where my faith was cultivated in the Word of God by these lovers and teachers of the Word, and I began to grow and mature in the faith. Not only from the teachings of my pastors but from other great teachers of the Word like the late Kenneth E. Hagin. In addition, my husband and I would catch the early Sunday morning telecast with Kenneth and Gloria Copeland before heading out to the Sunday morning service at our local church where we also served.

And on top of that, there was also the late Dr. Richard E. Eby, whom I only heard three times, but he deposited into me such deep things of the Spirit with his life and death testimony. Whether through conferences or books, these people of God captured my heart with their message of faith. They instilled within me a love for the Word. And this biblical teaching catapulted me into the realm of faith like no other. *"So then faith comes by hearing, and hearing by the word of God"* (Romans 10:17). Every one of these teachers of the Word taught me another element of faith.

It was in the mid-eighties, and the pastors invited a guest speaker by the name of Charles Capps. Once again, I found myself unlearned in this area, but still intrigued with regard to the message of the power of our spoken words. But this time another element was introduced to me, the prophetic power of God's Word spoken. I don't recall if the actual word *prophetic* was mentioned, but the concept and working of it was being taught.

After the service, the speaker was selling a little booklet of Scriptures on the back table. I picked up a copy and devoured it. I would use the faith Scriptures in this booklet in prayer and witnessed success in the power of the spoken word. Then over the years as my faith grew in the knowledge and revelation of the Word, so did my spiritual ability increase in the arena of the prophetic, especially in the realm of prophetic healing.

If you glean anything from my beginning to learn to live in the power of faith-filled words, I pray that you will see that I had a purpose within my heart to live in the realm of faith that would please God and bring about His glory.

It would be years later, after being on the mission field full time, that the following two men of God would minister volumes of mysteries of the Spirit to me through their writings—Lester Sumrall and Smith Wigglesworth.

I am a strong advocate for the power of the spoken word, and every word that we speak prophesies either life or death. And with the power of this revelation, I see the dead come back to life, incurable diseases healed, tumors disappear, blind eyes see, deaf ears hear, paralytics walk, and unusual and unexplainable miracles manifest. All of this and so much more, because I have learned how to wield the supernatural power of prophetic words that heal.

One of the key objectives of this work is to empower your words to create atmospheres that release supernatural healing to the entire being—spirit, soul (mind and emotions), and into the physical body.

People Are Empowered with the Law of the Spoken Word

God speaks forth in Genesis 1:26, *"Let Us make man in Our image, according to Our likeness."* Part of His likeness that He equips people with is the power and authority of the spoken word; whether you follow after Him or not, all spoken words have power, no matter who releases them.

God creates the world with the power of His faith-filled words. It's how He works—with words. He releases the power of His prophetic words throughout Genesis 1 and says, *"Let there be…"* and we know the history of creation, and there was…and He saw that what He creates with His faith-filled words is good.

> *Through faith we understand that the worlds were framed by the word of God, so that things which are seen were not made of things which do appear* (Hebrews 11:3 KJV).

His desire is that we emulate Him, mirror or reflect His image, with our words and prophetically create what we have need of. Romans 4:17 teaches us that we are to call those things, which do not exist as though they did. This is speaking of the vocabulary of the prophetic, Holy Spirit's language. And we can learn to emulate Him and speak healing and creative miracles like He does: *"A man will be satisfied with good by the fruit of his mouth…"* (Proverbs 12:14 KJV).

The Name It, Claim It Controversy

You may be balking already just reading the title of this section and thinking, *Are you one of those name it, claim it believers?* First let me say, I agree with you that there has been a lot of abuse and just plain greediness regarding this principle, but that doesn't mean we toss the law of the spoken word out the window. We couldn't change it even if we wanted to, it's His law. He put it into motion, and He's the same yesterday, today, and forever (Hebrews 13:8). God doesn't change (Malachi 3:6), and His laws remain the same.

What it does mean is that the Church needs to grow up and mature in this area. If we would get back to the basics of our faith, then we would desire what He does, which is to be about our heavenly Father's business and win people to Christ (see Luke 2:49). And even if some never repent of a greedy heart, that still doesn't stop the power of the spoken word. And regardless of what some may or may not do, prophetic healing is real, and it works. There are people all around the world crying out for healing, and God wills for them to have it.

He asks you to pick up your responsibility and open up your mouth and release prophetic healing, not so that you can make your temporal abode more comfy, but to bring increase to His Kingdom for His glory, not yours.

Can I get an amen?

But so that you do know that yes, God does care about your earthly desires as well, I want to share a sweet testimony of how the power of the spoken word works. Trust me, this is good.

Years ago in our children's home, I was talking with the little ones about what they would like for Christmas. After they shared their list of heart's desires, Joaquin, our now adopted, grown son said to me back then, "Mom, I want a merry-go-round." At first I thought, *Wow, now that's quite the gift. How are we going to swing this one?* But I thought about it again for a moment and said, "Okay, kids. Who wants a merry-go-round?" They all raised their hopeful hands in the air. "Let's pray and you ask Jesus for a merry-go-round. I'll believe with you." And with excitement in their voices they all asked Jesus for this special gift.

As parents, we need to teach our kids about the fun-loving side of Jesus and teach them how to believe right where they are. Hey, many teach them to write a letter to Santa Claus and make believe he listens and rewards their innocent beliefs and good behaviors. I figure how much more should we teach our children to believe in the real thing, Jesus, and teach them how to have faith for things that require big faith.

And yes, for all these little ones the merry-go-round was a big item to trust Jesus for. But we didn't just end it with a prayer of faith, we took it to the next level. For the next few days we gathered together and declared words of faith, "Thank You, Jesus, for a brand-new merry-go-round."

Our fun-loving Jesus so enjoys when His children—young and old and somewhere in between—activate this amazing gift of faith and speak with confidence to Him as if they believe He's real. He actually listens to them and cares about their wants and desires too. That it pleases Him, and He delivers their simple wish.

It wasn't but a few days later when I received an email from a family in Guatemala saying they would like to give a special gift to the children in our children's home for Christmas. And asking if I have a suggestion. Of course, I suggested a merry-go-round and they loved the idea, agreed to it, and then contracted someone to construct one and deliver it in time for Christmas.

But God doesn't just supply our wants, He actually places specific desires in our hearts. Psalm 37:4 says, *"Delight yourself also in the Lord, and He shall give you the desires of your heart."* Our fun-loving Jesus desires to exceed our wish list with His goodness toward us. *"Now to Him who is able to do exceedingly abundantly above all that we ask or think, according to the power that works in us"* (Ephesians 3:20).

And do you know what sweet Jesus does next?

A few days later, I received another email from a Sunday school class in the United States that wanted to do something extra special for the children—like build them a playground. Our God is so real, so good and it well pleases Him when we emulate Him and trust in His absolute goodness toward us.

So I ask you, is this just a bunch of blab it and grab it nonsense? Or is this evil of us to claim a blessing from our heavenly Father? Do the children learn a great lesson in faith that will lead them into a relationship of trust with a real God who truly listens? Does this request, that some say is selfish and earthly, lead them into a greater level of faith? Yes, it does. How about these little ones laying hands on the sick and watching the people be healed? This is right where the power of the spoken word leads children.

And if you are still critical about claiming a blessing from God, perhaps you should humble yourself like these children do and pray and thank Jesus for a merry-go-round. You might be pleasantly surprised. And I hope you have room in your backyard for one!

In the same way, let your light shine before others, that they may see your good deeds and glorify your Father in heaven (Matthew 5:16 NIV).

Return to Childlike Faith

Oh, if only God's people would humble themselves and return to childlike faith, believe every word He says, and not doubt His ways, what glory would shine from the Church today. Ponder upon a nursing baby. This child does not doubt or question Mom if she is able to give milk or not, or if she is willing to give milk. This faith-filled child without question readily receives what he or she needs. This is what childlike faith is like. It is the most powerful faith there is. It truly believes all the promises and receives all of the benefits that God has for them, because they do not doubt, but believe without question, so they easily enter into the Kingdom of God.

I find it sad that one day this nursing infant will be taught not to trust and will struggle to believe. It is the sins of the tongue such as lying, manipulation, and broken promises that are mainly responsible. You have to be taught not to trust, not to believe.

But His Spirit invites you to return to Him, trust His ways, do not doubt in your heart, believe Him, and readily receive all that He has for you.

While I was ministering to a woman, I saw the most loving vision I had ever seen before. In this vision, the woman seeking supernatural healing converted into an all-trusting, infant child. Jesus Himself picked her up, looked at her with such tender mercy, brought the infant up to His chest, and held her tight in the security and safety of His loving arms. I knew at that moment this woman believed and received her healing by faith.

The Spirit of Prophecy

The definition of "prophecy" according to Strong's G4394 is:

> a discourse emanating from divine inspiration and declaring the purposes of God, whether by reproving and admonishing the wicked, or comforting the afflicted, or revealing things hidden; esp. by foretelling future events. It is used in the New Testament of the utterance of Old Testament prophets, of the prediction of events relating to Christ's kingdom and its speedy triumph, together with the consolations and admonitions pertaining to it, the spirit of prophecy, the divine mind, to which the prophetic faculty is due. And the endowment and speech of the Christian teachers called prophets. And the gifts and utterances of these prophets, esp. of the predictions of the works of which, set apart to teach the gospel, will accomplish for the kingdom of Christ.[1]

To take on the spirit of prophecy is to accept Jesus at His word: *"For the testimony of Jesus is the spirit of prophecy"* (Revelation 19:10). He is the prophetic word confirmed, *"And so we have the prophetic word confirmed, which you do well to heed as a light that shines in a dark place, until the day dawns and the morning star rises in your hearts"* (2 Peter 1:19). While on earth, Jesus was well aware of who empowered Him and what His earthly assignment was. While in the synagogue, He was handed a scroll with Isaiah's writings, and He confidently read the following prophecy of Himself from Isaiah 61:

> *"The Spirit of the Lord is upon Me, because He has anointed Me to preach the gospel to the poor; He has sent Me to heal the brokenhearted, to proclaim liberty to the captives and recovery of sight to the blind, to set at liberty those who are oppressed; to proclaim the acceptable year of the Lord"* (Luke 4:18-19).

The Holy Spirit empowered Jesus to proclaim the truth with authority and to confirm His message of the Kingdom with signs and wonders, and the same Spirit strengthens us to emulate the work of Jesus on this earth: *"But you shall receive power when the Holy Spirit has come upon you; and you shall be witnesses to Me in Jerusalem, and in all Judea and Samaria, and to the end of the earth"* (Acts 1:8). Will you take Jesus at His Word and accept the spirit of prophecy?

Jesus Emulates the Father

> *Then Jesus answered and said to them, "Most assuredly, I say to you, the Son can do nothing of Himself, but what He sees the Father do; for whatever He does, the Son also does in like manner"* (John 5:19).

According to Hebrews 1:3, Jesus is the express image of the Father, and He upholds all things by the word of His power. He emulates His Dad. Whatever He says, Jesus says. What the Father does, He does. Jesus is not in competition and does not work independent of the Father. This proves the unity between Jesus and the Father and that they are one. And they do not work against one another, but with each other. And this is what we are to do as well. We are to do what Jesus does on this earth. We are to emulate Jesus as Jesus does the Father: *"Love has been perfected among us in this: that we may have boldness in the day of judgment; because as He is, so are we in this world"* (1 John 4:17).

> *God, who at various times and in various ways spoke in time past to the fathers by the prophets, has in these last days spoken to us by His Son, whom He has appointed heir of all things, through whom also He made the worlds; who being the brightness of His glory and the express image of His person, and upholding all things by the word of His power, when He had by Himself purged our sins, sat down at the right hand of the Majesty on high, having become so much better than the angels, as He has by inheritance obtained a more excellent name than they* (Hebrews 1:1-4).

We are to live out our faith, trust, and belief in the Father, just as Jesus did. The Father didn't just send His Son Jesus to sacrifice His life for a dozen men, but for *all*. And for *all* Jesus came to show how to live by this faith on the earth in the Father and His Word.

To start His earthly assignment, Jesus first called and showed twelve men by example how to live to be free from a religious spirit and to have a real, authentic relationship with the Father. And how to activate extraordinary faith for the benefit of others. Then He sent out a group of seventy by twos. *"After these things the Lord appointed seventy others also, and sent them two by two before His face into every city and place where He Himself was about to go"* (Luke 10:1).

And then Jesus reached out to the individual—us—and commissioned the true believer to emulate Him on this earth:

> *And these signs will follow those who believe: In My name they will cast out demons; they will speak with new tongues; they will take up serpents; and if they drink anything deadly, it will*

by no means hurt them; they will lay hands on the sick, and they will recover (Mark 16:17-18).

Four Steps to Emulate Jesus

1. First and foremost, you must be able to identify with Him. *"But as many as received Him, to them He gave the right to become children of God, even to those who believe in His name"* (John 1:12). In order to identify with Jesus, you need to align yourself with Him as Savior.

2. After you can identify with Him, activate His authority. *"Then He called His twelve disciples together and gave them power and authority over all demons, and to cure diseases"* (Luke 9:1). As a disciple of Christ, you have been gifted with His authority.

3. You speak like He speaks, full of the authority of faith. *"And so it was, when Jesus had ended these sayings, that the people were astonished at His teaching, for He taught them as one having authority, and not as the scribes"* (Matthew 7:28-29). Learn and say what He says and the way He speaks it.

4. Then you do what He does, live out faith-filled words. *"...Whatever He says to you, do it"* (John 2:5). You have to live your life according to His faith language.

How Does Jesus Release the Power of His Words?

If we are to emulate Jesus, the Living Word, then it would be a wise idea to study how He releases and utilizes the power of His words in the Scriptures. According to Luke 2:40, He grows in wisdom and grace. This word "wisdom" in Greek is *sophia,* meaning both worldly and spiritual intelligence and basically pertaining to every matter of life (Strong's G4678). And the Greek word for "grace" is *charis,* the manner or act of graciousness, especially the divine influence upon the heart and its reflection in the life (Strong's G5485).

Jesus releases and utilizes the power of His words with the anointing of the Holy Spirit (Luke 3:21-22, 4:14, 18-19). This anointing is to consecrate Jesus for the Messianic office and to furnish Him with the necessary powers for its administration (Strong's G5548: *chriō).*

Some Activities Jesus Can Do with the Power of His Words

With creativity, He creates the world we now live in (Genesis 1:1; John 9:6-7). He overcomes satan's temptations in the wilderness by quoting the authority of the Scriptures (Luke 4:1-13). He exercises authority over storms (Mark 4:35-41), demons (Luke 4:35-36), sickness (Luke 4:39), death (Luke 7:11-17, 8:40-56; John 11), and even to a lack of provision (Luke 5:4-6).

How Does Jesus Administer the Word of God?

Jesus teaches with authority and wisdom in the synagogues (Luke 4:15,32) and to the crowds (Luke 5:3). He teaches with parables (Matthew 13:24-50), preaches Kingdom principles (Luke 6:20-23), and demonstrates His Words with power (John 6:1-14).

How Does Jesus Deal with His Word?

With faith, Jesus heals sickness and incurable diseases. The Book of Luke is written by the hand of a physician named Luke, under the unction of the Holy Spirit, and is an excellent source for healing examples. Wherever He goes He heals the sick individual or ministers healing to the multitudes. He often ministers healing directly to the person or He sends His healing Word into the airways and the person is healed (Psalm 107:20; Luke 7:1-10).

How Does Jesus Minister with His Words Under Persecution?

We read throughout the Gospels how Jesus—while in the midst of illegal trials, false charges, cursings, insults, spittings, beatings, whippings, spikes hammering through His hands and feet, betrayal and abandonment by His disciples, and crowds demanding His immediate death—He holds His tongue, doesn't lash out, and keeps His emotions and tongue under submission. And at the end, He calls out to the Father, *"Forgive them, for they do not know what they do"* (Luke 23:34).

How Does Jesus Pray?

He takes the time and builds Himself up in prayer alone with the Father (Mark 1:35; Matthew 14:23; Luke 6:12, 22:41-44). He sets the example and teaches the crowd how they should pray to the Father as well:

> *Our Father in heaven, hallowed be Your name. Your kingdom come. Your will be done on earth as it is in heaven. Give us this day our daily bread. And forgive us our debts, as we forgive our debtors. And do not lead us into temptation, but deliver us from the evil one. For Yours is the kingdom and the power and the glory forever. Amen"* (Matthew 6:9-13).

And even now, while He sits at the right hand of the Father, He utilizes the power of His words and intercedes for us (Romans 8:34).

How Does Jesus Use Prophetic Gifts?

Jesus operated in the prophetic gifts while He walked the earth for thirty-three years. With the woman at the well, He revealed her hidden secrets through a word of knowledge, something that is happening in the present tense in John 4:17-18: *"The woman answered and said, 'I have no husband.' Jesus said to her, 'You have well said, "I have no husband," for you have had five husbands, and the one whom you now have is not your husband; in that you spoke truly.'"*

With a word of wisdom, Jesus tells His disciples part of a future event, *"Let these words sink down into your ears, for the Son of Man is about to be betrayed into the hands of men"* (Luke 9:44). It is not the total word, does not disclose all details, but gives part of the word to them.

Jesus utilizes the simple gift of prophecy, which is to edify and build up the Church and there is no future telling in this gift: *"These things I have spoken to you, that in Me you may have peace. In the world you will have tribulation; but be of good cheer, I have overcome the world"* (John 16:33).

And with His words He *prophesies* of future events to His disciples and tells them of the signs of the Last Days in Matthew 24.

When Jesus speaks, it is with a purpose. Sometimes He doesn't speak at all; but when He does, it cuts to the heart of the matter and His words of truth set people free in spirit, soul, and in the physical body. This is the beauty of the power of the prophetic.

The Reason We Can Release Prophetic Healing Power

While teaching at a healing seminar, the Lord revealed to me what was happening during the initial whippings that Jesus received at the whipping post. First of all, those beginning whips are softening the tough fibers of His flesh, like someone prepares a tough piece of meat. This whipping breaks down a physically strong body that is sustained by the power of faith, so that His body can soak in and marinate in the sickness and disease of all humanity.

But before His body can saturate this consequence of our perverseness and sin, He has to first give a verbal consent before the slaughtering process can begin. And He does this in the Garden of Gethsemane when He cries out, *"Father, if it is Your will, take this cup away from Me; nevertheless not My will, but Yours, be done"* (Luke 22:42). And because of these consenting spoken words, we can now release the power of prophetic healing. This is a great gift He gives to us and even a greater responsibility to uphold the Covenant of the Blood. Will we value His precious blood and prophetically speak forth healing?

The Hosea 4:6 Litmus Test

Time and time again there are certain Scriptures that the Lord continues to bring to my attention, to reveal to me my heart in a matter. Hosea 4:6 is one of these Scriptures: *"My people are destroyed for lack of knowledge...."*

In today's world, many of the hearts of God's people have waxed cold, and they have become stiff-necked and rebellious toward Him. Some remain unteachable, others will not spend a little effort to change the way in which they speak, and there's always a few who don't believe they have a problem to begin with—these are the ones who fail the test.

But then there are those whose hearts are pliable, teachable, and workable. And these are the ones who will move to the next level with the Spirit of God and release great moves of the Spirit around them. Will you be one of the pliable, teachable, and workable people who can launch into prophetic healing?

The Hosea 4:6 litmus test consists of two questions. To help identify where your heart is in the matter of the prophetic and healing power of your words, ask yourself these two straight-forward questions and answer honestly:

1. *Have I been speaking harmful words over myself and others because I truly did not understand the power behind them?*

2. *Or am I a rebellious child and I rebel against God's challenge to change?*

Like in the second part of Hosea 4:6: *"Because you have rejected knowledge, I also will reject you from being priest for Me; because you have forgotten the law of your God, I also will forget your children."*

Ouch! That hurts. Right? But what hurts more? The consequences of pain and suffering because we have been ignorantly speaking wrong words over ourselves? Or that we suffer because we refuse to change our negative ways? Or worse yet, our leaders do not care enough about us to rebuke our rebellion and lead us into the paths of righteousness?

Let's pray: *"Father God, forgive me because I did not understand the harm my negative words have been producing in my physical body or in the lives of those around me. Holy Spirit, take me down this journey of the prophetic and healing power of my words. I desire to be pliable, teachable, and workable to learn from You. In Jesus' name, I pray, amen."*

Take Action and Listen to Yourself

It's time to take action and listen to yourself speak. And when you hear a negative word or a faithless statement slip out of your mouth, retract its power from producing. How do you do this? Retract it from existence. Say aloud, *"In Jesus' name, I renounce that faithless statement."* And ask God to forgive you for saying something filled with doubt and unbelief.

And if you really want to learn, write the negative phrase down in a notebook. Then take a few moments and ask the Holy Spirit to teach you how to restate that comment so that it produces godly results in your physical body or situation. He wills to teach you. You just have to have a teachable spirit.

If we would only learn how to hold our tongues and use our words wisely, we would save ourselves from a whole lot of trouble. And this is the topic of the next chapter.

Personal Word Checkup

Am I willing to take the Kingdom of God by force if necessary? Do I struggle with this doctrinal position that our words have power? Am I able to readily receive my need from the Lord? Do I need to repent and return to childlike faith? Do I accept the spirit of prophecy in my life? Will I wield the power of my tongue to heal and protect my faith in God so that it is not rendered useless? Have I taken the four steps necessary to emulate Jesus? Will I emulate Yeshua, the Living Word, and in His likeness release prophetic healing by the power of my spoken words? Am I willing to take action and listen to the words I speak?

Group Discussion

What is one word or phrase that I caught slip out of my mouth this past week that I asked the Lord to forgive me for and to show me how to reword it so that it would release prophetic healing instead of negative results? How did He teach me to rephrase it?

Questions for Chapter 1— Emulate the Living Word

1. The remnant is rising, and what's on her tongue?

2. What is the enemy afraid of when it comes to the prophetic healing that he speaks lies about it among the Body of Christ?

3. With what does God create the world?

4. The language of the prophetic healing belongs to whom?

5. What is the most powerful type of faith?

6. What do we accept when we take on the spirit of prophecy?

7. What happened in the Garden of Gethsemane that we can now release the power of prophetic healing?

8. What should you do if you say something filled with doubt and unbelief?

Endnote

1. Prophecy, *Vine's Expository Dictionary;* https://www.blueletterbible .org/lang/lexicon/lexicon.cfm?strongs=G4394; accessed April 28, 2018.

CHAPTER 2

HOLD YOUR TONGUE

To gain a clear understanding of the prophetic and healing power we all possess in our tongues, we need to first learn how the negative and positive power of our daily words affect us and those around us. Before we can implement the use of our words in the spirit realm correctly to release prophetic and healing power, we need to start with the natural use of our words.

Word of the Lord

AND THE SPIRIT OF GOD WOULD SAY TO YOU, DEAR READER, *"If you would only trust Me when I tell you to hold your tongue, you would save yourself from all sorts of trouble. But how often I remind you, and yet you speak without control. I desire you to learn My ways. The benefits of My spiritual law of the spoken word are rich, limitless, and full of My favor; but in order for you to access this full power of the Spirit, you will have to cleanse yourself from the sins of the tongue. If you will, you will begin to walk in the fullness of the blessings of the Father as you were created to do."*

Hold Your Tongue

People often speak before they think and cause all sorts of detrimental effects to themselves and to others with the damaging power of negative speech. But this is not the Lord's desire for His people to speak foolishly. We are to learn to wield the power of our words, because in actuality they all prophesy life or death.

We need to learn the art of holding our tongues, refraining from saying some things, even though we might really want to or at times even be expected to, because either it will cause harm or it is just plain wrong to say. Develop this ability of restraint. This is especially true when it comes to choosing our words wisely. King Solomon writes in Ecclesiastes 3:7 from the NIV version of the Bible, when speaking of timing, he shares that there is *"A time to keep silence, and a time to speak."* We need to exercise God's wisdom, timing, and even more so, caution before we speak aloud.

Proverbs 15:23 (NIV) says, *"A person finds joy in giving an apt reply— and how good is a timely word!"* As we study and learn together, we will see that our words have great power to create and to destroy, and the situations we live in today are a direct result of our words spoken; whether out of wisdom or foolishness, we are living out our words that we thoughtlessly spoke out the other day.

Jesus exemplified the art of holding His tongue under extreme pressure for us in Isaiah 53:7, *"He was oppressed and He was afflicted, yet He opened not His mouth; He was led as a lamb to the slaughter, and as a sheep before its shearers is silent, so He opened not His mouth."*

We can gain further wisdom from James 3:1-12:

> *My brethren, let not many of you become teachers, knowing that we shall receive a stricter judgment. For we all stumble in many things. If anyone does not stumble in word, he is a perfect man, able also to bridle the whole body. Indeed, we put bits in horses' mouths that they may obey us, and we turn their whole body. Look also at ships: although they are so large and are driven by fierce winds, they are turned by a very small rudder wherever*

the pilot desires. Even so the tongue is a little member and boasts great things.

See how great a forest a little fire kindles! And the tongue is a fire, a world of iniquity. The tongue is so set among our members that it defiles the whole body, and sets on fire the course of nature; and it is set on fire by hell. For every kind of beast and bird, of reptile and creature of the sea, is tamed and has been tamed by mankind. But no man can tame the tongue. It is an unruly evil, full of deadly poison. With it we bless our God and Father, and with it we curse men, who have been made in the similitude of God. Out of the same mouth proceed blessing and cursing. My brethren, these things ought not to be so. Does a spring send forth fresh water and bitter from the same opening? Can a fig tree, my brethren, bear olives, or a grapevine bear figs? Thus no spring yields both salt water and fresh.

For example, your teenage son or daughter has a problem with sassing back. You have a choice to make, you can put the flames of rebellion out and refrain from responding in a negative manner, or you can set the forest on fire and go back and forth with flaming words fueled with anger, bitterness, and hate. God gives you the right to choose, but one promotes peace and the other—war.

Let's study the words of wisdom penned for us by the hand of the apostle James under the unction of the Holy Spirit, and see what the Spirit would have us do.

It's Wise to Control the Tongue

James 3:1-5 rightfully warns us:

My brethren, let not many of you become teachers, knowing that we shall receive a stricter judgment. For we all stumble in many things. If anyone does not stumble in word, he is a perfect man, able also to bridle the whole body. Indeed, we put bits in horses' mouths that they may obey us, and we turn their whole body. Look also at ships: although they are so large and are driven by fierce winds, they are turned by a very small rudder wherever the pilot desires. Even so the tongue is a little member and boasts great things. See how great a forest a little fire kindles! It's no easy task to control the tongue, especially under pressure like when your life is hanging in the balance, or your body is racked with physical pain and suffering. But this is the time you must exercise complete control and speak according to God's healing covenant to activate your spiritual rights and responsibilities as an ambassador to the King of kings. It's wisdom to hear and heed this message and educate yourself in the power of the spoken word and put it into practice.

And generally speaking, if you are physically spent it's best to go find a quiet place and get some rest, like Jesus did when He would escape from the demands of the crowds to be alone with the Father. Otherwise you are likely to say something that you will regret and have to mend later on. There is a time for silence, as long as it is not used to punish another.

However, the report went around concerning Him all the more; and great multitudes came together to hear, and to be healed by Him of their infirmities. So He Himself often withdrew into the wilderness and prayed (Luke 5:15-16).

According to the Scriptures, wise people are determined by their ability to control their tongues. Proverbs 10:19 says it this way, *"In the multitude of words sin is not lacking, but he who restrains his lips is wise."* Proverbs 17:27-28 is just as revealing, *"He who has knowledge spares his words, and a man of understanding is of a calm spirit. Even a fool is counted wise when he holds his peace; when he shuts his lips, he is considered perceptive."*

How Wise and Foolish People Differ in Their Speech

Undeniably, there is a big difference between the way in which the wise and the foolish people speak, but what's not always obvious to some are the results of their words. The words of the prudent are not released with fear, but with caution. They actually take a moment to think before they speak. And in doing so are able to respond to a situation, rather than just react negatively to one. There is a recognizable form of godliness on their tongue. They are courteous enough to give others the opportunity to express what's on their mind. And their speech is seasoned with the fruits of the Spirit, and a bountiful harvest in life the wise reap from well-spoken words.

While on the other hand, careless people speak recklessly. They tend to be people of many words, impulsive or hasty, and just blurt whatever comes to their mind. Spiritually they lack filters that can decipher from appropriate and inappropriate speech.

Words from the foolish are toxic and unsafe for the receiver. Their tongues drip with self and sin. They are inconsiderate and forget that the other person may want to respond; and when the other person can get a word in edgewise, they don't listen anyway, they just blab. It is a challenge to have any level of conversation with them. They reap the negative results of careless speech—unnecessary havoc and stress.

And during their time of need they wonder why God doesn't answer their cry for help. They fail to see that their excessive talk prevents them from hearing God's response, because they just speak right over Him as well. Ecclesiastes 5:2 (AMP) says it like this:

Do not be hasty with your mouth [speaking careless words or vows] or impulsive in thought to bring up a matter before God. For God is in heaven and you are on earth; therefore let your words be few.

Beware of the Foolish

Unfortunately, foolishness abounds in today's world, but you can learn to discern these people and protect yourself from the adverse results of their dialog. Whether they hold a public position in the world or within the Church or they are someone never seen or noticed or somewhere in between, they share several common traits. For one, they possess a lying, manipulative spirit and are never to be fully trusted. They are highly self-centered, plagued with the epidemic disease of "me, myself, and I." If they dish out a compliment, it is never to uplift the other person, but to gain some sort of favor or leverage over that person. There is always an ulterior motive behind their words. And often the receiver senses something wrong during the conversation but can't quite put their finger on it. But if you listen to their words carefully, you'll learn to discern the fault of foolishness within their words and protect yourself from the unfavorable consequences of their careless speech.

The Father of Lies

Someone once told me that a liar and a thief are of the same spirit and you cannot separate the two. This is exactly right, satan is a prime example of this fact. Jesus speaks to those who do not believe He is the Christ about the devil and who they and their actions are aligned with:

> You are of your father the devil, and the desires of your father you want to do. He was a murderer from the beginning, and does not stand in the truth, because there is no truth in him. When he speaks a lie, he speaks from his own resources, for he is a liar and the father of it (John 8:44).

Jesus calls him the thief who comes to steal, to kill, and to destroy; see John 10:10. And he repeats the same tactic over and over again against us. The first order of action is with the power of words—he lies. When it comes to sickness and disease, he and his evil work force whisper lies to our minds. Lies filled with fear, symptoms, doubt, and unbelief. And as soon as we buy into his lies, he swoops in with action and these lies manifest in our mortal bodies.

How to Correctly Deal with Satan's Shenanigans

Instead of reacting to foolishness with foolishness, or sin with sin, how should we respond with words of wisdom? In the case just mentioned, respond as Jesus does when He is being tempted in the wilderness by responding with God's Word, and God's Word alone. Don't enter into a conversation with him and his demons—use the authority of God's Word against him. He recognizes the authority of God's Word, so you silence him and put him in his place, under your feet.

My advice is to not bite into his bait; and if you already have, spit it out. I've just told you how to do this, but now for a little instruction on what you should say. Next time he taunts you with a hostile medical report and lying symptoms, you rebuke him saying:

> I rebuke you, satan. I command you to be silent in Jesus'
> name. No! I do not accept this disease. I do not have it. It
> does not belong to me. Jesus purchased my healing with His
> own blood and gave to me all of His authority to silence you
> from releasing your word curse over me. In the name of Jesus,
> I do not have this disease because I possess His healing power
> and by His stripes, I am healed (Isaiah 53:5).

Does this mean the enemy will immediately stop? Probably not, he didn't stop after his first attempt against Jesus in the wilderness, and he probably won't stop after the first attempt against you either. You are going to have to effectively enter into spiritual warfare with the enemy. And in the beginning it will be a war with words inside your mind. He will badger you to try to get you to release those negative thoughts with your spoken words. But if you will stand your ground, hold up your shield of faith, use the sword of the Spirit, wear your helmet of Salvation, shod your shoes with the Gospel of Peace, and wear the belt of truth, you will win this battle with the enemy. You will wear him out just like Jesus did with the power of faith-filled words.

Let's look at another real-life situation that I have had to face while in the ministry dealing with the devil's shenanigans or just plain people's foolishness, and how did I rightly respond to the situation with the power of my words.

One young teacher—whom I honestly loved, but due to inexperience in a place of authority working with adolescent boys—just did not want to abide by the rules. The rules were in place to protect both student and teacher. This teacher would overstep the bounds and take the adolescent boys from wayward backgrounds outside of the classroom without permission, and where no one could see them. I was the overseer in this situation and I had to uphold the boundaries. She did not like this and rebelled against my God-given authority over her. I had to have a time of words with her in the office. She finally looked up at me and with all sincerity of heart, she shouted at me three very destructive words, "I hate you." I stood up and walked over to her and replied with equal sincerity, "Yes, but I love you." My response was real, genuine, from my heart, and it stopped satan's wickedness dead in his tracks.

God's Word teaches us that love covers a multitude of sins (1 Peter 4:8). And one way we express love is with our words. But like I mentioned, these words need to be real, genuine, from the heart; and when they are, they silence satan, put an end to his shenanigans, and even the foolishness of people.

How was I able to calmly respond to this young teacher's hateful words? I spent much time in prayer over this young lady. And all those spoken words of faith in prayer had already healed my soul, my mind, and my emotions from her rebellion.

Do Not Enter into Conversation with the Devil

The devil is a mastermind at trickery with words. He always looks for ways to make God's people fall. Let's journey all the way back to the Garden of

Eden when the devil disguises himself as a talking serpent. Apparently during this time, the serpent has legs and does not slither, but walks. He sees Eve's weakness, she doesn't fully understand who she is. How do I know this? Because this is the very thing he uses to confuse and tempt her with. Read this encounter:

> *Now the serpent was more cunning than any beast of the field which the Lord God had made. And he said to the woman, "Has God indeed said, 'You shall not eat of every tree of the garden'?"*
>
> *And the woman said to the serpent, "We may eat the fruit of the trees of the garden; but of the fruit of the tree which is in the midst of the garden, God has said, 'You shall not eat it, nor shall you touch it, lest you die.'"*
>
> *Then the serpent said to the woman, "You will not surely die. For God knows that in the day you eat of it your eyes will be opened, and you will be like God, knowing good and evil"* (Genesis 3:1-5).

The devil starts to converse with Eve, she listens and enters into conversation with him. But she is of an innocent nature, she doesn't know how to lie, doesn't even know what he is up to. And as usual that serpent of old takes advantage and tricks her with his words. He tells her if she eats of this tree she will be like God. He tells a lie, she already is like God, not equal to Him, but created in His mirror image. Because she enters into conversation with him, she falls for his lie and reaps serious consequences for listening to him.

What Happens to the Lying Serpent?

But there is something here that I believe we miss, and it is a great lesson for us. This lesson has to do with God's response to this lying serpent. What does He take away from the serpent?

So the Lord God said to the serpent: "Because you have done this, you are cursed more than all cattle, and more than every beast of the field; on your belly you shall go, and you shall eat dust all the days of your life. And I will put enmity between you and the woman, and between your seed and her Seed; He shall bruise your head, and you shall bruise His heel" (Genesis 3:14-15).

According to these Scripture verses, God takes away the serpent's legs, his feet, and his ability to walk—now it has to slither on its belly and will eat the dust of the earth. Let me teach you what is prophetically happening here.

The sixth time Jesus sheds His atoning blood for us is through His feet. Feet in the Bible represent authority, and when Jesus releases His blood through His feet, He gives to us the ability to walk in His authority on this earth.

And because the serpent allows satan to use him to harm Eve, Adam, and us for this matter, God steps in with His authority and removes the serpent's feet, ability to walk, and lowers his rank of authority. And not only will it slither on its belly, which is a sign of disgrace, but what does God declare it will eat? The dust of the earth. Let me ask you, "What does God use to create Adam with? What does the human body return to after the spirit leaves the body?" Again, the answer is the dust of the earth.

Here we see the hateful nature of satan and the jealously he feels toward Adam and Eve and toward us too. Why? Because we are created in the mirror image of Elohim, no other creation is created as we are, not even the angels. And as I teach you in my first work, *DARE to Believe* in chapter 1, the devil is just a fallen angel. And we have been given authority over him. God refers to him as the Serpent of Old.

Now what has me jumping here is this—the devil, the serpent of old, because of his lying, wicked nature, and the misuse of the Law of the Spoken Word, and because of the sin of his mouth used to harm us, God takes and fills satan's mouth with our dust, our remains. It's part of the prophetic fulfillment of your enemy losing his rank in the scheme of eternity. And when satan uses his words against you and tries to trick you from activating your authority against him, like your heavenly Father, you can put him in his place. Take the heel of Yeshua and stomp on the serpent's head and boldly declare, "As He is, so am I on this earth, and I have been given authority over you and your wicked works, including this disease. I will not return to dust before my time. You are disgraced and on your belly you go. But remember, you will eat my dust."

Word of the Lord

THE WORD OF THE LORD TO YOU CONCERNING THAT SERPENT OF OLD, *"Did I not tell you to be aware of that serpent of old? Now why he acts so bold, is just a trick to be told. As the last days events unfold, you will find out what he sold. The mold of his soul is not a sight to behold. And it's not worth all the world's gold. Cold is the soul that falls into his flaming hold."*

What Would have been the Correct Response to the Serpent?

What would have been the correct response to the serpent in the Garden of Eden? And how will this help you to respond to ungodly situations?

Both Adam and Eve should have recognized the ungodliness of the words of the serpent. Yes, they were not exposed to evil, they didn't understand what it was, and more so the negative consequences they would reap with aligning themselves with evil. But what they did have going for them was the ever-presence of God. They knew only truth and the goodness it produces. Spiritually speaking, they should have known that something wasn't lining up to the truth.

Case in point: when banks train their workers to recognize counterfeit bills, they do not handle false bills, they only examine true bills. It works the same way in the spiritual realm, when you read and study the Word of

God and live out His Kingdom ways, you easily discern satan's counterfeit, just like a banker can quickly identify a false bill from a true bill.

And when it comes to discerning the intents and words of people, if you abide in God's abode and train yourself in His Word, you will have that check inside of you when someone is trying to pull a fast one on you. But you first must handle the truth in order to recognize the lie. This is such an important lesson for these last days we are living in now.

What should Adam and Eve have done in this situation? They both should have taken their authority, called out satan, and walked away from him. And this is exactly what you should do when you find yourself in a questionable situation.

Right Words Bridle the Whole Body

Just like a bit inside a horse's mouth causes it to obey your commands, so do right words spoken bridle the whole body. Your physical body obeys your spoken words. It does exactly what you tell it to do. Therefore, think before you speak. What do you have need of? Do you need healing and strength? Then you speak words filled with healing and strength. Solomon, who is sought after for his great wisdom, teaches us that *the tongue of the wise promotes health*" (Proverbs 12:18).

If you speak words that rebel against God's healing promises, then your physical body will follow after the direction of your unhealthy words and will spiral downward into sickness and disease. It may take time to bring your body under submission to your new healing vocabulary. But even though it may rebel at first like a wild horse, eventually it will learn to come under the submission of that newfound bit and it will eventually obey your commands.

I like how the Native Americans taught their horses to submit to their authority. They led them into the nearby lake or river and climbed up upon their back. It was less painful for the horse and rider as the water would break the power of the horses' resistance. So too, submerging yourself in the Living Water will break the wild will of your tongue much quicker.

Your Tongue Is the Rudder

In Mark 4:35-41, we read the account of how Jesus calms the storm.

On the same day, when evening had come, He said to them, "Let us cross over to the other side." Now when they had left the multitude, they took Him along in the boat as He was. And other little boats were also with Him. And a great windstorm arose, and the waves beat into the boat, so that it was already filling. But He was in the stern, asleep on a pillow. And they awoke Him and said to Him, "Teacher, do You not care that we are perishing?"

Then He arose and rebuked the wind, and said to the sea, "Peace, be still!" And the wind ceased and there was a great calm. But He said to them, "Why are you so fearful? How is it that you have no faith?" And they feared exceedingly, and said to one another, "Who can this be, that even the wind and the sea obey Him!"

When you learn to steer your ship correctly, you will speak forth words of power that cause the fierce winds of sickness and disease to dissipate. You have been given the true Captain's authority over all sickness and disease, *"Behold, I give you the authority to trample on serpents and scorpions, and over all the power of the enemy, and nothing shall by any means hurt you"* (Luke 10:19). Learn to use Jesus' authority and dominate satan with faith-filled commands.

There is a saying, "Loose lips sink ships"; this phrase was coined as a slogan during World War II as part of the US Office of War Information's attempt to limit the possibility of people inadvertently giving useful information to enemy spies. The slogan was actually *"Loose Lips Might Sink Ships."* This was one of several similar slogans that all came under the campaign's basic message: *"Careless Talk Costs Lives."*[1]

Careless words spoken create great devastation on the human body as well. The information gained by your enemy, satan and his demonic force, will be the very tactics used against you. And it's your negative words spoken that give them the ammunition they need to openly attack and sink your ship. These negative words can cost you your life.

Quite frankly, many Christians have loose lips that sink ships—in fact, they sink entire fleets. If you will open up your spiritual ears and listen to what is being spoken from most pulpits today, you would understand that the Spirit of God is giving you a warning, trying to teach you to avoid being shipwrecked.

God's ill-informed people, especially leaders, continue to say, "It is not God's will to heal all people, but destines some people to be sick so that they can dedicate more time to study the Scriptures and reach out to the sick and hurting more effectively." This is satan's rubbish! It's false doctrine against the blood of Jesus that He so painfully shed at the whipping post so that people can be healed from all sickness and disease. It devalues the power of the blood. It's also a weak excuse to not search out God's Word and learn how to have faith to heal.

Instead of repeating satan's lies, it would be best to be honest with yourself and with others and admit that you do not understand God's healing power as you should, but you are willing to learn how to have faith to heal.

Let's pray: *"Father God, forgive me for aligning myself with the enemy against Your healing power. I admit I have been ignorant in this area of faith and caused great harm against myself and others. Forgive me for the sins of doubt and unbelief. Holy Spirit, teach me how to have faith to heal, in Jesus' name, amen."*

The Tongue Defiles the Whole Body

Even so the tongue is a little member and boasts great things. See how great a forest a little fire kindles! And the tongue is a fire, a world of iniquity. The tongue is so set among our members that it defiles the whole body, and sets on fire the course of nature; and it is set on fire by hell (James 3:5-6).

Learn from the Scriptures and extinguish the wicked fires of your tongue. In the natural, before a forest can be set ablaze it needs to be tinder-dry and extremely flammable. Let's compare this to the condition of your spirit-being. If you're dried up spiritually, your faith is weak and you're in a spiritual drought. And because you lack the Word of God, there's a shortage of Living Water that comes from your spirit. Therefore, you become careless, loose-lipped, and you speak evil things about others and over yourself. This is the reason your physical body is weakened and cannot standup against satan's fiery darts of sickness and disease. And the body is easily destroyed because of your ill-spoken words.

In our own strength it is next to impossible to cleanse our tongues of negative and poisonous word curses, but with God it is possible—and in the next chapter we will learn how to do so.

Personal Word Checkup

Do I think before I speak? Am I able to control my tongue even under pressure? Do I utilize my words wisely? Or do I speak foolishly? Do I tend to answer satan, or do I put him in his place? Do my words rebel against God's healing promises? Do I have loose lips? Do I tend to sink ships with my words? Do my words defile my body? Am I willing to learn from the Scriptures and get a handle on my tongue?

Group Discussion

From the readings of this chapter, how can my tongue defile my physical body? Are there any particular areas I need to adjust?

Questions for Chapter 2—Hold Your Tongue

1. We are to learn to wield the power of our words, because in actuality they all do what?

2. What must you do when your life is hanging in the balance, or your body is racked with physical pain and suffering?

3. What do the wise reap from well-spoken words?

4. What are the negative results of careless speech?

5. The foolish are highly self-centered and plagued with what epidemic?

6. The first order of satan's action against us is with what power? How does he use those words?

7. Why should we not enter into a conversation with the devil?

8. What must you handle first in order to recognize a lie?

9. What will happen to your physical body if you speak words that rebel against God's healing promises?

10. What can your negative words cost you?

Endnote

1. The Phrase Finder; http://www.phrases.org.uk/meanings/237250 .html; accessed April 4, 2018.

CHAPTER 3

NEGATIVE AND POISONOUS WORD CURSES

Word of the Lord

A WORD FROM THE LORD FOR YOU, *"You open up your mouth and without thought just pour out a blessing and with the same breath pour out a curse. And oftentimes this is done without rhyme or reason, and this can lead to spiritual treason. But you are at the edge of a new season, and together let's set to reason and start to believe in Me again."*

Is it true that "Sticks and stones may break my bones but words will never hurt me"? Small children chant this when they are on the defense. But is this really true? No, it's not true. Words have the power within themselves to destroy or restore, to make sick or to heal, to weaken or to strengthen. Stop and think before you speak. Do you want to reap what you say?

When you hear someone badger children saying, "You're good for nothing," they will discover ways to prove that person right. And their cruelty and negative words are to blame for the trouble. Likewise, if you habitually confess, "I'm just a poor person." What will you become? You will be poor.

By your own mouth you curse your family's finances. Proverbs 23:7 says, *"For as he thinks within himself, so he is."* And Matthew 15:18 reveals the end result of negative thinking, *"But those things which proceed out of the mouth come from the heart, and they defile a man."*

Take another situation, a woman continues to nag, "I am so sick and tired…" How will her body respond? Eventually it will catch up to her ill use of words, and her body will be sick and tired. By the power of her own words she wears out her physical strength and destroys her health.

What happens when a husband and wife constantly tear each other down with words of insults? They become hurt, angry, and bitter toward one another. And eventually they destroy their relationship. Proverbs 15:1 tells us that harsh words stir up anger. And Proverbs 18:19 says, *"A brother offended is harder to win than a strong city…."*

Negative words hurt you and others, and sometimes the damage is almost irreversible. Choose your words well and heal, instead of hurt.

What Are Word Curses?

Curses are unfavorable utterances verbalized to ravage destruction upon another person. They come in various forms with different levels of toxicity. Most often, people are unaware of the word curses that proceed from their mouths. But then there are those who are fully aware of what they do, and intentionally desire to harm you.

Unintentional Word Curses

A man is not feeling well and goes to the doctor for a check-up. He hears the report that his blood pressure is very high. Instead of just telling the man the results and that they are going to work with him to bring it down, the doctor speaks words of death and demonstrates with actions that this man will have a heart attack or a stroke. The conversation goes beyond reporting results and the doctor unintentionally prophesies death.

How should this man respond to the doctor's colorful report? After all, he did seek the doctor out for medical advice. How about, "That's not going to happen to me. I will do what it takes to bring this blood pressure down to normal levels. Will you help me do this?"

Another man was told he was going to die of kidney disease. This man firmly said, "No, I am not going to die." And he's alive and well.

Another person is told they will never walk again. This one said, "I do not receive that. I will walk again." And he did.

Intentional Word Curses

Then there are those who are intentionally cursing others with evil, such as in this situation. One lady from the United States shares that her neighbor openly practices witchcraft and hates her because she knows she is a Christian. They live in a city in Minnesota where the houses are built very close together. This woman's neighbor made a voodoo doll in the resemblance of her and stuck pins in the heart and made other demonstrations of her death and hung it outside the door so she would see it daily.

What do Christians do in this situation? First of all, use the power of the spoken word and declare, "I have a blood covenant with the Father, and every curse has been broken, including this one. And in Jesus' name, your evil works have no effect on me." And in addition, I suggest you hang a simple plaque in the shape of a heart on your door with the following message, "Jesus loves you." They will be angry at first, but it's a simple message that will speak into the depths of their spirit. God's Word does not return void, see Isaiah 55:11. Also, pray for their salvation, only Jesus can redeem them from hell and themselves.

> But I say to you, love your enemies, bless those who curse you, do good to those who hate you, and pray for those who spitefully use you and persecute you (Matthew 5:44).

One of my readers wrote, "A woman called me and said that someone has put curses on me. She also said in order to remove the curse I will need to send her 700 US dollars. Have you ever heard of such a thing?"

More and more Christians are confronting this situation now. And with greater reason, it is very important to clearly realize what Jesus did for us. He undid the power of the curse when He shed His blood for us at Calvary. It's crucial to take action and learn how to muscle your authority in Jesus' name and say "No" to the enemy and all of these curses. You do not need to pay anyone money to break these word curses—Jesus already paid the price and broke the curse with His shed blood. And this is the truth of the matter.

> *Christ has redeemed us from the curse of the law, having become a curse for us (for it is written, "Cursed is everyone who hangs on a tree")* (Galatians 3:13).

People who flagrantly practice the occult are joining their negative forces against everyday Christians, pastors, and other people who hold a position in the church or over our government officials to cast spells or curses to do us harm. What do we do? We pray in faith for one another, and for our leaders against these blatant attacks of the enemy through these lost souls enslaved to the devil and occult practices.

> *Praying always with all prayer and supplication in the Spirit, being watchful to this end with all perseverance and supplication for all the saints* (Ephesians 6:18).

> *Therefore I exhort first of all that supplications, prayers, intercessions, and giving of thanks be made for all men, for kings and all who are in authority, that we may lead a quiet and peaceable life in all godliness and reverence* (1 Timothy 2:1-2).

I share again with you a real-life situation that I personally encounter with a witchdoctor in Northern Tanzania in my first work, *DARE to Believe* on pages 257-258, who tries to curse me with death. But he does not get very far with his wickedness; instead, when he lightly brushes against me, he goes flying backward through the air and lands dead on the ground. I quickly make my way through the crowd to go to him, and when I touch him he feels cold and stiff as if he has been dead for a very long time. A lady in the crowd whispers in my ear, "Do you know who he is?" I answer her quickly, "No. Who is he?" She says, "He's the witchdoctor." As soon as I hear her words, the Holy Spirit brings to my remembrance my prayer that morning, "And may every curse and assignment that the witchdoctors try to put on us this morning, may they bounce back on them and teach them a lesson to leave us alone."

What was the curse this witchdoctor cursed me with? Death. Did he succeed? No. Why not? Because I voice activate my authority as a true believer in Yeshua, and I have been quoting since I was a baby Christian: *"No weapon formed against me shall prosper. No evil will come near my dwelling. Every lying tongue set on fire against me will be exposed, silenced, and brought to shame in Jesus' name."*

Then, standing over the dead witchdoctor, in the all-powerful name of Yeshua and with life-giving words, I called the lost man back to life.

What to Do When They Can't Verbally Respond

Suppose you, or a loved one, are in the midst of a fiery trial and can't think of what to say or are unable to speak because fear is taking over, or physically you are too sick or hurt. What should you do? Cry out the name of your Lord, "Jesus, Jesus, Jesus…" How can you do this if you can't speak? Before the spirit leaves the physical body, you can still hear. You can even see, and see more than you can with your physical eyes.

If it is a loved one, speak to the person like I do. I give instructions to individuals while on their deathbeds who can no longer respond to repeat the name of Jesus over and over again. At first glance, it looks as if the person does not respond, but as we pray in the Spirit and exercise the supernatural fruit of patience, we observe the tongue starts to move, slowly at first, but surely it is moving. How? They start to call on the name of the Lord in the spirit realm. And within moments, we can hear a faint whisper of the mighty name of our Lord, Yeshua. And the power of the name brings the person back to life.

The Name of Jesus Is Torturous to Demonic Forces

I find the name Jesus spoken with authority is highly torturous to satan and his demons. I have even seen satan crawl into a garbage can and try to hide from me as I proclaim the name that is above every other name, Jesus. (You can read this testimony in its entirety in my second work, *Greater than Magic* in Chapter 1, pages 27-28.) As I minister healing and deliverance, I hear demons beg me to stop using the name of Jesus against them. But I expose their secret to you—they cannot withstand the pressure of His name. Therefore, use the name of Jesus liberally and with all authority.

Believers Cursing One Another over Doctrinal Differences

Then there are Christians who fight against one another because they do not agree doctrinally in all things. I love what the healing power of the Lord does for people, but some people are not willing to believe. What do I say? "If you change your mind, you let me know and I will minister to you." And I pray on my way out, "Lord, help them to see the truth in Your healing power." I do not have to argue with these people. That never does any good anyway.

I often have visiting pastors from different denominations who come to hear and judge the message I am teaching at healing conferences. They and their congregations have need for physical and emotional healing, and before they invite me to come, they check out what I have to say and what I believe. Most often these pastors come to me after a session in total amazement—saying that they have never heard this message taught before, or that they have not seen it for themselves in the Word.

My point is this, I do not fight doctrine with people, nor do I compromise my faith in any way. Rather, I systematically teach these seekers the Word concerning prophetic healing and allow them the grace, time, and space to come to grips with this message. It's a lot to accept when you realize that as a pastor, you and your congregation have missed out on God's healing benefits because you, the leader of the flock, were taught a faithless doctrine, and you willingly believed it and know that many have suffered for your lack of understanding of Jehovah Rapha's healing power.

And to the pastors who read this message, I do not curse you. I applaud your willingness to listen and learn something you have not understood before. And I pray that our heavenly Father will pour out a blessing that you are not able to contain or keep to yourself and many will be delivered and healed within your congregations for His glory and honor.

Earlier in the year, at a healing seminar in Florida, a visiting pastor came forward in the prayer line and his opening words were a confession and a plea for prayer for healing. He was not taught these things about the Holy Spirit and everything he heard during the weekend was all new to him—and all that he heard taught witnessed into the depths of his spirit.

Personally, as I write this, my spirit grieves for him and the others who were taught in seminary to not only minister, but to live without the power of the Holy Spirit. Their hearts want to serve, but their hands are bound to false doctrine and are unable to help. We who were blessed with the teaching of the Holy Spirit need to have hearts of compassion for these people and reach out to the ones who are willing to listen and learn.

> *With it we bless our God and Father, and with it we curse men, who have been made in the similitude of God. Out of the same mouth proceed blessing and cursing. My brethren, these things ought not to be so. Does a spring send forth fresh water and bitter from the same opening? Can a fig tree, my brethren, bear olives, or a grapevine bear figs? Thus no spring yields both salt water and fresh* (James 3:9-12).

Christians Blessing and Cursing God at the Same Time

This is a painful topic to write about, but I must shed light on a serious matter that is affecting the relationship between God and His people. And it is not God's fault. It is the sin of the people who doubt His promises.

They join the congregation and lift up hands and release blessings to God as they sing beautiful harmonious songs filled with tender lyrics of worship, and then they turn around and complain to their neighbor about how bad their situation is. They confidently lift up the power of their suffering, the strength of their disease, and will declare curses with their mouths that their God is not willing to heal His people anymore.

Imagine being a parent and your children praise you for cooking, cleaning, and tending to their simple wants and desires, except they fail to believe your basic promises to them. In fact, they run around the neighborhood and evangelize the area with the message that you once were really good and did all these marvelous wonders for them, but now you no longer care for their basic physical health needs. In essence, this is what is being proselytized by many people about our Lord. I ask you, "Is this the Good News that will draw all people to Him?" Do you see how we can bless and curse God at the same time?

The Cursed Effects from Abusive Speech

We have all said things from time to time that we wished we hadn't, and even though the words are wicked, a heartfelt apology, encouraging words, and a little time is usually what's necessary to undo the damage. But what about abusive speech that spills out of an evil heart over and over again?

An unloving parent tells their children repeatedly that they will never amount to anything. Guess what? Those words are accursed, and it does not take long for those children to reach that goal. These types of words have lifelong damaging effects.

Along with a lot of love and assurance, it will take deliverance and transformation in the Word of God for hurt individuals to overcome the curse of these words. But with willing hearts, they can heal and overcome.

What about the Curse of Passive Parenting?

A Christian couple sits back and watches their young teenagers entangle themselves in outright rebellious, ungodly, and often occult music, movies, and books—and they wonder where they went wrong. The answer lies in the power of the spoken words, and in this case with the parents' lack of them. They choose the passive route and say nothing. And so the enemy takes advantage of the parents not speaking up and uses all means of warped entertainment to enslave their listeners and readers to the evil power of their message. And the whole while their Bibles are sitting on a nearby shelf collecting dust for the past several years. With the Word of God, they could have the blessing of better-behaved children, but instead they settle for the curse of passive parenting and their family is paying a heavy price for it all.

Generational Curses of Sin

You shall not make for yourself a carved image—any likeness of anything that is in heaven above, or that is in the earth beneath, or that is in the water under the earth; you shall not bow down to them nor serve them. For I, the Lord your God, am a jealous God, visiting the iniquity of the fathers upon the children to the third and fourth generations of those who hate Me, but showing mercy to thousands, to those who love Me and keep My commandments (Exodus 20:4-6).

When sin is not repented of it effects people around us; and in this case, it goes from family member to family member. So the next time you think your sin is not having an effect on others, think again—it is. And it always does.

Look at alcoholism, which finds its way from one generation to the next if it is not confronted and dealt with spiritually. In our children's home in Guatemala, we would have to attribute the suffering of all the children to the root of alcoholism of the birthparents. And through our authority, we teach these children to break off this sin by repentance and not repeat the lifestyle. It is the only way to free your future generations from its wickedness.

Some people do not believe in generational curses because Jesus paid the price to redeem us from the curse by becoming the curse for us. And yes, this is absolutely true, but He also redeemed us from hell, but we first have to activate this power of redemption by faith in His atoning blood and then we have to use the power of our words and verbally express our faith with confession.

Generational Curses in the Form of Sickness and Disease

Breaking generational curses in the form of sickness and disease works the same; we have to first believe in the healing power of the blood to break the generational curse from disease, such as breast cancer. But when we do, we activate the atoning whips with the power of the spoken word: "In Jesus' name, I am redeemed from this generational curse, and I am healed. I do not have breast cancer. I am strong and healthy and will live long for the glory of my Lord."

The Cursed Power of Labels

Alcoholism is a strong label, so too is autism. What comes to your mind when you hear these labels and others such as cancer, dyslexia, and epilepsy to name just a few? You probably think of life-long or life-ending incurable diseases and situations. What type of feelings do you struggle with when hearing these labels? Anger, confusion, depression, fear, and hopelessness are common and natural feelings that come with these labels and others. But God doesn't look at you with a label on your head. These are human ways of classifying satan's wickedness.

What happens when we invite God into the situation? Let's find out. For starters, remove the power behind these labels and add the words, "Delivered and healed from _____ in Jesus' name."

Alcoholism, the world says, "Once an alcoholic, always an alcoholic." This is only true if you believe it and speak it out. Because once you put your faith in it, you will either live it out for yourself, or you will hold another in bondage to this label. I know of many people who no longer are alcoholics, my husband is one of them. The day he surrendered his life to

Jesus, he was delivered from the fear and shame this label held over him. And alcohol no longer called to him.

You see, alcoholism is not a disease, it's a sin, and a demon is behind its stronghold. But once you repent of your sin to the Father and receive Jesus as your Redeemer, you have a blood covenant that breaks the bondage to this sin, and you are free to walk away from it.

Autism is a scary label for a parent to hear spoken over their child. And this creates great fear and anxiety within the family. But my God is bigger than this label. Our adopted son, Andres, was labeled with severe autism. But through prayer and fasting and searching the Scriptures concerning deliverance and healing, he has been set free, completely delivered and healed from this. Our faith in the redemptive blood of Jesus healed him and made him whole.

No matter the label, Jehovah Rapha, the God who heals, is always greater, more powerful. You have to decide which label you will put your trust in—the name of the disease or healed by the blood of Jesus.

The Silent Curse of Passive Faith

Passive faith is a silent killer. Yes, there is a time to be silent, but there is also a time when we need to speak up. And when it comes to the devil, you better use the power of prophetic healing and stop his wickedness against you and your loved ones. Refusal to do so will kill you. Because you lack conviction and boldness to take a stand of faith, he will take advantage of your fear and silence and assume complete control and do what he does best—steal, kill, and destroy you and those you love. See John 10:10.

Word of the Lord

THE WORD OF THE LORD WOULD SAY TO YOU, *"You will take time to cleanse the plate, but what about that spirit of hate. Be careful before it is too late, guard that gate, and don't swallow satan's bait. Rate your eternal fate, know that I have set the date, and soon you will no longer have to wait."*

Society's Hate Speech

In today's society, the tongue of the people has become so vial and deadly. It is full of hate toward everyone. It is critical, demanding, full of gossip, openly lies, unforgiving and vengeful in every way.

Christians cannot afford to enter into satan's evil schemes of the tongue. Why not? You defend your right to free speech, and yes, you do have the right to speak your mind, but there are spiritual consequences for aligning yourself with the enemy. We need to consider the price of our words.

According to the Word, faith operates by love, and love alone. There are no exceptions to God's rules. And one way we demonstrate love is with our words. *"For in Christ Jesus neither circumcision nor uncircumcision avails anything, but faith working through love"* (Galatians 5:6).

For those of us who call ourselves disciples of Christ, there is only one option for us to take, and this is repentance and forgiveness. You say, "I can't forgive them." If you don't, then you can't heal either. As usual, unforgiveness holds the unforgiving individual in bondage to the curse of satan, and the curse crosses into every corner of our lives—spiritually, emotionally, mentally, and physically.

As a follower of Yeshua, are you allowed the luxury to hate? According to the Gospel of Luke, no, you are not. *"But I say to you who hear: Love your enemies, do good to those who hate you, bless those who curse you, and pray for those who spitefully use you"* (Luke 6:27-28).

Does God make room for you to act out with vengeance? Romans 12:19 in the Amplified Version of the Bible says, *"Beloved, never avenge yourselves, but leave the way open for God's wrath [and His judicial righteousness]; for it is written [in Scripture], 'Vengeance is Mine, I will repay,' says the Lord."*

And no matter how painful the situation, there is only one way that's acceptable for believers—repentance and forgiveness. There is no other way. Let's hold unforgiveness up to the light of God's Word.

> *Let all bitterness, wrath, anger, clamor, and evil speaking be put away from you, with all malice. And be kind to one another,*

tenderhearted, forgiving one another, even as God in Christ forgave you (Ephesians 4:31-32).

Take heed to yourselves. If your brother sins against you, rebuke him; and if he repents, forgive him. And if he sins against you seven times in a day, and seven times in a day returns to you, saying, "I repent," you shall forgive him (Luke 17:3-4).

For if you forgive men their trespasses, your heavenly Father will also forgive you. But if you do not forgive men their trespasses, neither will your Father forgive your trespasses (Matthew 6:14-15).

Hate speech is dangerous, and you will not walk in God's blessings. The consequences of this sin will eventually catch up to you. Heed the word of the Lord in the opening of this chapter, *"Be careful before it is too late, guard that gate, and don't swallow satan's bait."*

Common Examples of Poisonous Speech with Healing

To help highlight what I mean by the poison of the tongue, I've added three common examples of poisonous speech when it comes to healing.

A man is suffering in the hospital from a second bout with cancer. His pastor comes to call on him and says, "Well ya know, God is testing your faith again." This type of poisonous speech causes this patient to turn away from God in his time of need. How can he confidently go to God for help when he is told, by a member of the clergy that God is responsible for his cancer? There is no comfort or encouragement in such words. And because of this type of false doctrine, this man does not believe God wills to heal him and he dies.

A woman writes, "I believe, and yet nothing happens." As long as this lady continues to confess that nothing happens, nothing *will* happen. She's trapped by the poison of her own words. And just because she does not see immediate results does not mean healing does not happen. But with the negative release of doubt, she undoes the power of faith-filled words for healing, and she continually has to push the restart button and start all over.

I was having this conversation with a group and the example of the fig tree came up. Even though Jesus curses the fig tree, the effects of these words are not visible to the natural eye until later as the work begins at the roots where the eye cannot see. But the work is done at the release of the prophetic word. For example, when we curse cancer at its root and we do not see the immediate results, because it is inside the body, like the roots of the fig tree are underground where the natural eye cannot see. But with faith in the prophetic word spoken, the cancer has to obey, dry up at the roots, die out at the initial seed, and lose its power over us. This is another reason why we need to learn how to use our words correctly.

Another frequent example of poisonous speech is, "Healing happens in Africa, but it doesn't happen in the United States." Number one, this statement of unbelief is not true, God is not geographical, His healing power manifests wherever there is a believing heart. Number two, people are healed every day in the USA. But if you continue to speak this way, you will curse your area and you personally will not enjoy the healing power of the Lord.

Common Scenario of Poisonous Speech in Action

Here is an all-too-common scenario of a poisoned tongue among God's people. A member of God's family is suffering, fighting for his life, and several people come to call on the inflicted to pray for him. They walk into his room, stand at the bedside, and even pray a great prayer of faith and encourage him to stand strong and believe. It's a wonderful thing to do and actually we are called by God to do so.

Matthew 25:37-40 explains it this way:

Then the righteous will answer Him, saying, "Lord, when did we see You hungry and feed You, or thirsty and give You drink? When did we see You a stranger and take You in, or naked and clothe You? Or when did we see You sick, or in prison, and come to You?" And the King will answer and say to them, "Assuredly,

I say to you, inasmuch as you did it to one of the least of these My brethren, you did it to Me."

But as soon as they step out of the room, they release the devil's poison to the others in the waiting room and start to speak forth a deadly report. They forget that even though the patient can't hear them—Jesus does. And, so does the entire supernatural force around them. With these poisonous words of doubt and unbelief, ministering angels are hindered and destructive powers of demons are released.

Difficult but Not Impossible

For every kind of beast and bird, of reptile and creature of the sea, is tamed and has been tamed by mankind. But no man can tame the tongue. It is an unruly evil, full of deadly poison (James 3:7-8).

Naturally speaking, it is very difficult, next to impossible to rid our tongues of poisonous speech; but according to Jesus, we have His assurance that *"With men this is impossible, but with God all things are possible"* (Matthew 19:26). With God's help, we can cleanse our tongues from satan's poison.

Let's pray: *"Dear Holy Spirit, I am trusting in You to teach me how to overcome this unruly beast in my mouth. I stand upon Your word that promises that even though it is practically impossible for people to overcome the evil of the tongue, with You it is possible. And with Your help I will overcome and learn to heal and not poison myself or others with my words. I thank You for your faithfulness to help me. In Jesus' name, I pray, amen."*

Are you ready to learn some more?

Every Word Counts

In the supernatural, every word counts. Not only do words count in the supernatural realm, they produce in the natural realm once spoken aloud.

This also includes muttering to yourself. A spoken word is a spoken word, no matter the volume.

I know you may struggle with the fact that every word spoken counts, especially if you are a person of many words, or you love to joke around with people. If you will take time to listen to what you say, you will find this to be true, most jokes are highly negative and degrading, and they do harm to the listener. Oftentimes a jokester will joke themselves right out of a relationship. They just go too far.

And if you are one who talks without stopping to take a breath, I challenge you to take this problem to the Holy Spirit. Yes, it is a problem, a control issue. It's not healthy communication. Communication involves sharing and exchanging news and information with one another. With an excessive talker, there is no communication taking place. It's a one-way dialogue, which is wrong and sinful as well. It may even be demonic.

Your words have power, and every word you speak matters.

The Pattern of Poisonous Speech and the Scriptural Remedy for the Cure

1. *Poisonous speech always starts with ungodly thoughts, being careless of what we put into our minds.* How does this ungodly thought process begin concerning sickness? The thoughts begin through your visual and auditory senses. One way negative thoughts get into your mind is via negative media advertisements, such as the Internet, television, radio, and magazines. Sickness and symptoms are declared into the airways and then announced is a miracle drug to cure it. Next, all the horrific side effects are cited and you ponder upon the report. And without thinking clearly, you fall into the trap and agree and accept the symptoms and the disease, and the side effects from the drugs.

There is a remedy for this found in Second Corinthians 10:4-5, *"For the weapons of our warfare are not carnal but mighty in God for pulling down strongholds, casting down arguments and every high thing that exalts itself against the knowledge of God, bringing every thought into captivity to the obedience of Christ."*

Learn to immediately respond aloud, "No, I do not accept this sickness and its symptoms into my body, in Jesus' name."

On the practical side, in our household, when watching a soccer game on the television and they break for commercials, our television is immediately shut off or the volume is turned off. You may think that is very radical, and you are right—it is. We actively take a stance against negative advertisements and their effects upon our lives.

2. *Ungodly thoughts transform into unhealthy desires and speech and contaminate us.* As you ponder upon their negative reports filled with disease and suffering, you begin to speak these matters out of your mouth and your sick-filled words begin to produce in your body. Matthew 15:18 explains it this way, *"But those things which proceed out of the mouth come from the heart, and they defile a man."* And as mentioned earlier, the spiritual remedy for contaminated speech and spirit is found in Philippians 4:8, *"Finally, brethren, whatever things are true, whatever things are noble, whatever things are just, whatever things are pure, whatever things are lovely, whatever things are of good report, if there is any virtue and if there is anything praiseworthy— meditate on these things."*

3. *Unhealthy desires convert into sin.* When you fill yourself with this constant barrage of sickness and disease, you begin to accept their terrible reports and doubt God's healing promises, and sickness overtakes your body. James 1:15 calls it as it is, *"Then, when desire has conceived, it gives birth to sin; and sin, when it is full-grown, brings forth death."* There is only one remedy for a cure from sin, repentance. Acts 3:19 instructs us, *"Repent therefore and be converted, that your sins may be blotted out, so that times of refreshing may come from the presence of the Lord."* And this is exactly what you need, the sin of doubt and unbelief forgiven and blotted out, so that His refreshing power can take over your body.

Recognizing this pattern of poisonous speech can help you avoid reckless speech altogether, but what can you do if your speech has already been contaminated? Is there a spiritual remedy or cure for this?

Heal Poisonous Effects with the Prophetic Power of Words

Let's read and learn how the prophet Elisha cleansed a poisonous pot of stew in Second Kings 4:38-41:

> *And Elisha returned to Gilgal, and there was a famine in the land. Now the sons of the prophets were sitting before him; and he said to his servant, "Put on the large pot, and boil stew for the sons of the prophets." So one went out into the field to gather herbs, and found a wild vine, and gathered from it a lapful of wild gourds, and came and sliced them into the pot of stew, though they did not know what they were. Then they served it to the men to eat. Now it happened, as they were eating the stew, that they cried out and said, "Man of God, there is death in the pot!" And they could not eat it. So he said, "Then bring some flour." And he put it into the pot, and said, "Serve it to the people, that they may eat." And there was nothing harmful in the pot."*

The negative report is that there is a famine in the land, but Elisha takes a stand against the circumstance and releases the power of his words and sends his servant to prepare a pot of stew for his hungry guests, the sons of the prophets. The sons of the prophets are the children of those called to speak forth messages, words for God. They're the fruit, good or bad, of spoken words by their fathers. They go out and gather herbs and gourds from a wild vine and his servant prepares and serves the fresh stew to them. But as they begin to eat it, they spit it out and cry out to the man of God that the stew is bad, poisonous to eat, and filled with death.

It's obvious to me that they are immature in the faith and have to call out to the man of God to fix the problem. Now, Elisha has a choice to make. He can just throw out the pot of stew and let his guests go hungry, or he can exercise the power of prophetic words and actions. He chooses the latter and fixes the situation, but not in the manner that they figured.

Instead of disposing of the bad stew, he healed it from the poison with his prophetic words and actions.

And this is what the Spirit desires for you to do, exercise your faith and heal the situation, the sickness or the disease by the power of your spoken words. Let's continue with the outcome to find out what takes place.

I find it interesting what he throws into the stew to cleanse it from the poison. He adds a handful of flour, or cornmeal—a base ingredient needed to make bread. I ask you, "Who is the Bread of Life?" Jesus is. What does the Word say concerning Jesus and healing? Jesus says of Himself in John 6:35, *"I am the bread of life. He who comes to Me shall never hunger, and he who believes in Me shall never thirst."* And healing is the children's bread referred to in Matthew 15:26-28.

Perhaps, the negative report is that your body has been poisoned with sickness or disease. What do you do? You need to throw a handful of spiritual flour from the Bread of Life with the power of faith-filled spoken words into the situation. And as if you are making a pot of stew in the natural, you need to add other spiritual ingredients such as the fruits of the Spirit—love, joy, peace, longsuffering, kindness, goodness, faithfulness, gentleness, self-control (Gal. 5:22-23). The final ingredient you will add is some action of faith; you need to stir your pot of miracles so that it does not burn but turns out well.

What I am teaching you in a creative way is that yes, the man or woman of God is here to help guide and direct you, even release the power of the miracle into you, but you have a part to play as well. Ultimately, you are responsible to bring your healing about. Jesus is very clear about this, He says, *"Your faith has healed you"* (Mark 5:34 NIV). And He says this to people over and over again.

One of the most life-changing ingredients of faith God has given to you is the power and authority of your own spoken words. As we study biblical healing, we will find confirmation after confirmation that God wills to heal His people, and He starts by healing the venomous tongue.

In this chapter, we've discussed negative and poisonous word curses and the problems they produce in our lives. Now, in this next chapter we are going to study about releasing the power of blessing of the tongue.

Personal Word Checkup

Have I been speaking poisonous words over myself? Have I been caught speaking word curses, whether intentionally or unintentionally? Am I claiming generational sin or sickness and disease? Have I accepted and acted upon a negative word label? Do I curse others who don't share my beliefs? Am I blessing and cursing God at the same time? Is my speech abusive to others? Do I tend to be silent when I should speak up? Have I fallen into the sin of society's hate speech? Do I speak venomous words that hinder my healing and affect my well-being?

Group Discussion

Discuss how you should respond to a negative medical report with your physician and with others? As a group, come up with verbal responses. Write these down and practice saying them aloud together. And if you have the time, talk about how Christians can bless and curse God at the same time.

Questions for Chapter 3—Negative and Poisonous Word Curses

1. What are word curses?

2. How should Christians respond when someone tries to put an intentional curse upon them?

3. What name should we call upon when we are in the midst of a fiery trial and can't think of what to say, or you are unable to speak because fear is taking over, or physically you are too sick or hurt to respond?

4. Along with a lot of love and assurance, what two things will someone need who has been verbally abused?

5. As discussed about the passive parents and their wayward children, where is the problem?

6. Why can't Christians afford to participate in any form of hate speech?

7. Why, when visiting a family member or friend in the hospital, do we need to be especially careful with poisonous words of doubt and unbelief?

8. In the supernatural realm every word counts, what happens with spoken words in the natural?

9. God wills to heal His people. What does He first heal?

CHAPTER 4

THE CREATIVE AND POSITIVE BLESSING OF WORDS

Words are spiritual tools that when used for God's glory cause the heavenly realm to manifest on the earth.

Word of the Lord

I, THE LORD, WOULD SAY TO YOU, *"Create and bless with your words. Don't refrain from sharing My grace with those all around you. With wisdom and favor impart a blessing that they cannot contain. My Word will not return void to you."*

According to the Scriptures, your tongue is full and overflowing with supernatural power. And this power is unleashed every time you open your mouth to speak. Spend a few moments and contemplate the following.

Spoken words are very important; in essence, they dictate the direction of your life. So choose them wisely. They can be a positive or negative influence, cause others to feel good or bad, happy or sad, they encourage or discourage, promote peace or hostility, they build up or tear down, heal or hurt, they create or destroy, and they always produce life or death.

Five Ways the Positive Force of the Tongue Can Release Healing

1. Declare praises to Jehovah Rapha and His faithfulness to keep His healing promises. *"Bless the Lord, O my soul, and forget not all His benefits: who forgives all your iniquities, who heals all your diseases"* (Psalm 103:2-3).

Declare: I give praise and glory to You, Jehovah Rapha, for Your faithfulness to keep and honor Your healing promise to me, by Your stripes I am forever healed. Because of the power of Your blood, I live a life that is full of health and strength. No longer am I weak, because You are strong in me. And by Your resurrection power, this premature death has been eradicated from within.

2. Produce supernatural healing with the power of prophetic words, *"(as it is written, "I have made you a father of many nations") in the presence of Him whom he believed—God, who gives life to the dead and calls those things which do not exist as though did"* (Romans 4:17).

Declare: I will not die, but live and testify of Your great goodness toward me. Nothing harmful may grow inside or on the outside of my body. My blood is washed clean and made whole. My immune system heals itself the way God intended it to.

3. Encourage trust to believe for God's miraculous ways, *"Trust in the Lord with all your heart, and lean not on your own understanding"* (Proverbs 3:5).

Declare: My trust is in Jehovah Rapha and in His healing power. I do not rely upon medical reports and results to dictate the state of my well-being. By my faith in His healing virtue I am healed and made whole.

4. Deny ownership of sickness and disease by claiming the power of the blood of Jesus. *"I shall not die, but live, and declare the works of the Lord"* (Psalm 118:17).

Declare: By the power of His blood and the promise of His Word, I am healed and made whole. In the name of Jesus, I do not receive this death report. No, my healing is bought and paid for in full at the whipping post.

Jesus shed His blood so I can walk while on this earth in the abundance of His life-giving blood.

5. Guard the body from sickness and disease by prohibiting its entrance. *"No weapon formed against you shall prosper..."* (Isaiah 54:17).

Declare: I decree supernatural protection around my physical body, and none of satan's mass weapons of destruction, including any form of sickness and disease, may enter into my body. I am strong and healthy, and illness cannot possess me, nor rob me of my life; in Jesus' name, I am protected.

The Power of Pleasant Words

Proverbs 16:24 shares insight to the power of positive words and the physical effects they have upon our minds, emotions and bodies when spoken. It says, *"Gracious words are a honeycomb, sweet to the soul and healing to the bones"* (Proverbs 16:24 NIV). This word "healing" in Hebrew is *marpe'* and it means health, remedy, cure, sound, wholesome, curative, medicine, a cure, and deliverance (Strong's H4832). Gracious or pleasant words possess healing properties and we should lavish one another with them.

Words that edify impart grace to the hearers. Read Ephesians 4:29 in its entirety, *"Let no corrupt word proceed out of your mouth, but what is good for necessary edification, that it may impart grace to the hearers." Oikodomē is the Greek word for "edification" (Strong's G3619), and it simply means to build up. Do our words build one another up? When they do, we impart grace, God's favor, charis (Strong's G5485), "upon each other."*

According to these two verses, grace or pleasant words have the power to heal the soul, the mind, and the emotions, which aligns with the Living Word, Yeshua's power in Isaiah 53:4-5 where it says that *"He carried our sorrows,"* meaning He bears both physical and mental pain. And because of the atonement, our spoken words of faith also carry this same healing property. So harness the power of pleasant words so you and others can heal.

If your friend receives a negative report that he or she will never survive this medical situation, be the bearer of encouragement and share God's healing report with them. Reassure them that the medical field does not have the last word in the situation—Jesus has the last word when He cries out on the cross, *"It is finished!"* His plan of redemption is complete, nothing is left undone, and healing has been bought and paid for by His blood. Prophesy words of healing into your friend's physical body.

Is the Power of Your Faith Limited?

Our enemy, satan, has led many to believe that their faith is limited in what they can do concerning their healing. But is your faith limited? No, it's not, and here are three biblical reminders of its limitlessness. And your healing is under the control of your tongue.

> *And He [Jesus] said to him, "Arise, go your way. Your faith has made you well"* (Luke 17:19).

> *Death and life are in the power of the tongue, and those who love it will eat its fruit* (Proverbs 18:21).

> *For assuredly, I say to you, whoever says to this mountain, "Be removed and be cast into the sea," and does not doubt in his heart, but believes that those things he says will be done, he will have whatever he says* (Mark 11:23).

We will be studying these verses and more throughout this work.

The Present Tense of Faith

> *"Now faith is the substance of things hoped for, the evidence of things not seen"* (Hebrews 11:1).

It is also important to learn how to use the proper tense of speech when declaring healing power over your body. What do I mean by this? When you say, "I believe God will heal me," you are speaking future tense and the healing does not manifest, because you cannot catch up to the future. The future is always in the realm of tomorrow. That's why God says in Hebrews 11:1 that faith is now. Let's look at "Now Faith."

Now Faith

Knowing that faith is in the present tense of now will change the way you pray and make your petitions known. Instead of crying out to the Lord and questioning when will He heal you, you will now walk in the revelation knowledge that you have already been healed (Isaiah 53:5). And instead of begging, you will be thanking Him for your healing before it manifests.

What might a prayer of thanksgiving with *now faith* sound like? *"I thank You, Jesus, for You are my Healer. You shed Your precious blood for me at the whipping post to purchase this cancerous tumor from my lungs. By these bloody whippings this tumor is already healed. I do not lay claim to this wicked disease. I decree I am already healed, in Your most holy name, amen."*

How to Approach God

Time is very short and we do not have time to waste with words of unbelief and doubt. And while I'm at it, let me tell you the truth—all your whining, crying, and begging God does not move Him. Only faith is pleasing to God, and this is how we are to approach God with a petition, *"Let us therefore come boldly to the throne of grace, that we may obtain mercy and find grace to help in time of need"* (Hebrews 4:16).

You are to:

- Come boldly before Him.

- Be confident in your identity in Him.

- Exercise His authority He gave to you over the situation.

- Thank Him that you are already healed by His blood.

The Battle with Goliath

In First Samuel 17:1-44, we read about the time of war between the Israelites and the Philistines. Both armies are standing on opposite hills ready to engage in battle. Every day the Philistine army sends out their champion warrior, Goliath. Every day this prized champion sends forth a challenge to the Israeli army that echoes across the valley:

> *Then he stood and cried out to the armies of Israel, and said to them, "Why have you come out to line up for battle? Am I not a Philistine, and you the servants of Saul? Choose a man for yourselves, and let him come down to me. If he is able to fight with me and kill me, then we will be your servants. But if I prevail against him and kill him, then you shall be our servants and serve us* (1 Samuel 17:8-9).

Goliath, the Mean-Fighting-Machine, is known and feared for his size and strength. He is the champion. The one everyone dreams of defeating, but dares not step into the ring with. Who will become his next victim?

The day of the Super-Heavyweight Final has arrived, and the stakes are high. Will the Israelites become enslaved to the Philistines? Who will accept Goliath's challenge?

The champ is fully decked out with his state-of-the-art armor and weapons. His very presence intimidates everyone. In fact, after taking one look at Goliath they all run and hide. He wants to fight one-on-one. He has complete confidence in his size and skill and knows he will conquer whoever steps forward. He is ready and waits for a striking battle. Who will fight Goliath?

Goliath becomes angry when he sees who the Israelites send out to fight him. Before him stands a young shepherd boy who walks the fields with the lambs and the sheep. What does he know about fighting? Now, this is the size mismatch of all time. Goliath can see the headlines now: "Champion Giant Slaughters Shepherd Boy." What a disappointing fight this will be for his spectators and utterly unfair for the young boy. He lets out a disgusted howl toward David "Am I a dog, that you come to me with sticks?" (See First Samuel 17:43.) But nevertheless, Goliath will fight. He tries to intimidate the young boy with his trash talk and threatens, *"Come to me, and I will give your flesh to the birds of the air and the beasts of the field!"* (See First Samuel 17:44.)

Perhaps, you are in a raging battle with the goliath, satan. You can learn from David's example of fearlessness and overcome satan's trash talk and intimidation.

But David, the shepherd boy with his slingshot in hand, fearlessly rises to the occasion, accepts the challenge, ignores the obvious, and with full confidence in His God replies to Goliath's threat:

> *"You come to me with a sword, with a spear, and with a javelin. But I come to you in the name of the Lord of hosts, the God of the armies of Israel, whom you have defied. This day the Lord will deliver you into my hand, and I will strike you and take your head from you. And this day I will give the carcasses of the camp of the Philistines to the birds of the air and the wild beasts of the earth, that all the earth may know that there is a God in Israel. Then all this assembly shall know that the Lord does not save with sword and spear; for the battle is the Lord's, and He will give you into our hands."*
>
> *So it was, when the Philistine arose and came and drew near to meet David that David hurried and ran toward the army to meet the Philistine. Then David put his hand in his bag and took out a stone; and he slung it and struck the Philistine in his forehead, so that the stone sank into his forehead, and he fell on his face to the earth. So David prevailed over the Philistine with a sling and a stone, and struck the Philistine and killed him. But there was no sword in the hand of David. Therefore David ran and stood over the Philistine, took his sword and drew it out of its sheath and killed him, and cut off his head with it. And when the Philistines saw that their champion was dead, they fled* (1 Samuel 17:45-51).

How does David activate the power of His words here? For starters, he activates the power of the name of the Lord, and then he boldly prophesies what is about to take place. And he confidently can speak forth such bold prophetic utterance because he knows the battle belongs to his God. After making his declaration of faith, he takes action, pulls back on the slingshot, and releases his faith. The small stone flies through the air and hits his enemy right smack-dab in the middle of his forehead. The mighty terror falls on his face to the ground, dead! David then picks up Goliath's sword and chops off his head. As the Philistine army sees what happened to their prized champion, they flee as fast as they can, and David, the shepherd boy, becomes the new world champion!

I know your enemy, the goliath satan, is bearing down hard, and he is fully equipped with the latest and up-to-date weapons of premature death. And these weapons have fearful names like AIDS, ALS, cancer, diabetes, Lyme's disease, and the like—and each one comes with its own petrifying death report that is both frightening and overwhelming. You may feel like the underdog in this fierce battle against your life and the odds are against you for survival, but let's learn from David's mighty victory of faith.

Goliath's sword was constructed of the strongest materials available at the time, but prophetically speaking, the enemy's sword consisted of words filled with fear tactics and insults to cause David to doubt his identity with the Lord of hosts, the God of Israel. The Word is clear *"For the thing I greatly feared has come upon me, and what I dreaded has happened to me"* (Job 3:25). In all my years in the healing ministry, I see the spirit of fear first comes to call; and if invited in, then comes the spirit of death. Be careful what report you listen to and who you allow to enter in.

What was David's weapon constructed of? Probably a single, long strip of leather or woven wool with a central "pocket" for the stone. From the outside looking inside, this was his weapon of warfare, and centuries later it doesn't sound like much. But we are to *"Be diligent to present yourself approved to God, a worker who does not need to be ashamed, rightly dividing the word of truth"* (2 Timothy 2:15). And when diligent to study, we discover facts that dare our faith. As I have here.

Prophetically we will analyze this—the sling is equal to our faith, and the swing motion represents when we put our faith into action. But like David, we need to become skillful in the way we activate our faith, and this is what we are doing in this work about the prophetic and healing power of our words. We can become mighty in the way we throw and aim our rocks. We can also be confident in our sling, our faith, because of the ammunition our sling is loaded with. David chooses five smooth stones. With a spiritual magnifying glass, look closer at the strength of the stone.

The Strength of David's Weapons

When I write, I like to investigate details to share with you in greater depth just how powerful this weapon of faith is, and we are zeroing in on the strength of prophetic healing. In my findings, we might want to readjust how we size the five little stones David took with him into battle.

> Archaeology confirms that slingstones were among the most important weapons in an ancient army's arsenal.
>
> At one excavation site in Israel (Khirbet el-Maqatir, 10 miles north of Jerusalem in Israel's West Bank), slingstones have been found in almost every area of the dig. These stones don't talk, but they do tell tales about the people who once lived there.
>
> "After three seasons of excavation, we have found nearly three dozen slingstones. Most are roughly round and slightly over two inches in diameter, from the size of a billiard ball to a tennis ball." —the Khirbet el-Maqatir dig director, archaeologist Dr. Bryant Wood (Associates for Biblical Research)
>
> Not naturally rounded, they all have evidence of tooling. Their size and shape suggest an early period in the Land of Israel's history. Larger slingstones, such as these, were generally used in this region prior to the Greek period (late 4th century B.C.).[1]

These do not sound like harmless little stones to me. And the slinger needs to be a skillful shot as David.

I love how archaeology confirms the Word; even though it may not be the intent of the archaeologists, it still does: "Archaeology confirms that slingstones were among the most important weapons in an ancient army's arsenal." And spiritually speaking, our ability to wield the strength of "The Slingstone" determines the outcome of every battle we face on this earth.

Christian, you have an even greater weapon in your sling, "Jesus, The Slingstone, The Rock." And regardless of the size and strength of the goliath in your life, you've got what it takes to slay it. You pull back, aim right for the center of its forehead, and let your faith loose—and that giant will tumble down!

Why Five Stones?

Do you ever wonder why David chose five stones, not just one stone or four stones or six stones? With a little study, you can discover what the number five means, and why it is prophetically important for you today that he has exactly five stones, and not another number. "The number 5 symbolizes God's grace, goodness and favor toward humans."[2] This is precisely what David needs, God's grace, the unmerited favor of God, to take Goliath down. And he has it, and so do you. If you will learn to wield *The Stone,* you will have brilliant strength to bring down to the ground the giant that is taunting you with trash reports. And the victory will amaze your onlookers and frighten your enemy.

Goliath's Weak Spot

Goliath is fashioned with state-of-the-art armor. But even with all of latest in human technology and reasoning, he is still vulnerable. Where is he vulnerable? His forehead is exposed. This presents David an opportune moment that will launch him into victory, provided he has the smarts and the wits to seize the moment. And as it turns out he does have what it takes, and so do you.
Goliath's forehead is not covered, meaning his vital organ, the brain that controls his entire body is not protected. And just one strike from the stone is all that it takes to bring the enemy down.

The enemy always has a weak spot, and with the wisdom of the Holy Spirit we can find it. Somewhere in his plan of destruction against us there's an opening for us to strike back. And depending upon our position, we will either be on the defense or on the offense where we can actually strike first. But in either position, we can ask the Spirit to reveal to us the location of this advantage point for us.

One major weak spot that the enemy always has is that he lies. And lies are a weak foundation. They are like sinking sand. Accepting his lies is like grabbing hold of his hand, and when you do, he takes you down into the sinking sand with him, and he suffocates and destroys you. But no matter what lie the enemy tries to use against you, you still have the advantage over him if you choose to voice activate the truth of God's Word—the mind of Christ.

The enemy does not have the mind of Christ, we do. The moment we accept Jesus as our Savior, we receive this amazing weapon of God's Word. And it is filled with very powerful weapons that satan does not possess—hope, love, joy, and peace to name a few. And this is what we will learn to wield and use against the enemy. The mind of Christ vocalized wins every time.

> *But the natural man does not receive the things of the Spirit of God, for they are foolishness to him; nor can he know them, because they are spiritually discerned. But he who is spiritual judges all things, yet he himself is rightly judged by no one. For "who has known the mind of the Lord that he may instruct Him?" But we have the mind of Christ* (1 Corinthians 2:14-16).

Ray Perkins and His Family Slay the Giant of Death

Ray Perkins goes in to the hospital for open heart surgery, but things do not go as planned. During the operation, his heart stops and the surgery cannot be completed. His chest is left open until he is stable enough for them to complete the surgery. They take him to the ICU and he is there for more than 40 days. He is connected to an ECMO machine to keep him alive, but the family is told that only 15 percent of the people on this type of life support actually survive. The medical reports are not good, death is ever present, but his family and friends accept the challenge and stand up to this goliath. And even though the situation appears impossible, they begin to release their faith, renounce death, and release life. And they bring down this giant spirit of death. Ray is alive and well and gives glory to God for what Jesus does for him.

Five Steps to Empower the Tongue

1. ***To spiritually empower your tongue, you must first be born again.***

> *Jesus answered him, "I assure you and most solemnly say to you, unless a person is born again [reborn from above—spiritually transformed, renewed, sanctified], he cannot [ever] see and experience the kingdom of God"* (John 3:3 AMP).

Wait a minute, didn't I boldly write in Chapter 1 that "all spoken words have power, no matter who releases them"? Yes, I did. And yes, all words do produce what they say, but we want to tap into the prophetic and healing power of our Lord and produce according to *His* will, not man's will.

2. ***After you receive Jesus as your Savior, you are ready for the baptism in the Holy Spirit to empower your spiritual vocabulary in His Kingdom ways.***

> *Listen carefully: "I am sending the Promise of My Father [the Holy Spirit] upon you; but you are to remain in the city [of Jerusalem] until you are clothed (fully equipped) with power from on high"* (Luke 24:49 AMP).

When you pray in tongues, you allow the Holy Spirit to pray through you the perfect will of the Father. Holy Spirit never prays against the Word of God, He always aligns Himself with it. So do you when you pray in your spiritual language.

3. ***Transformation by the power of God's Word is a must to power up spiritually.***

For the word of God is living and active and full of power [making it operative, energizing, and effective]. It is sharper than any two-edged sword, penetrating as far as the division of the soul and spirit [the completeness of a person], and of both joints and marrow [the deepest parts of our nature], exposing and judging the very thoughts and intentions of the heart (Hebrews 4:12 AMP).

The Word of God cuts to the chase and gets right to the heart of the matter. It convicts and reveals what has to change and directs the way to do so.

4. ***Don't just read the words of Christ, live what He says.***

But prove yourselves doers of the word [actively and continu-ally obeying God's precepts], and not merely listeners [who hear the word but fail to internalize its meaning], deluding your-selves [by unsound reasoning contrary to the truth] (James 1:22 AMP).

If the Word says to believe, then you believe. If it encourages you to activate your faith, then you put your faith into action. If it instructs you to speak life, then you use words that produce life.

5. ***When you say things that are mean and hurtful, repent.***

If we [freely] admit that we have sinned and confess our sins, He is faithful and just [true to His own nature and promises], and will forgive our sins and cleanse us continually from all unrigh-teousness [our wrongdoing, everything not in conformity with His will and purpose]" (1 John 1:9 AMP).

Do what's right and ask for forgiveness. In doing so, you release yourself from the devil's bondage and the consequences of the sin of unforgiveness.

Creative Force of a Faith-Filled Tongue

Faith is creative (see Genesis 1:1). It skillfully uses the power of the spoken word—like an artist paints with a brush in hand—and with creative words spiritually paints them perfectly in place.

A man stands before me during a healing service, tears run down his face as he shares his situation. He is an artist and he sculpts beautiful statues for a living. But he is now completely blind in one eye and losing his sight in the other. He simply cannot create without his eyesight.

I look at the man and say, "The Lord gives you your artistic talent, and His will is that you create for His glory." I lay my hands upon his eyes and immediately he can see.

A young lady can no longer taste food, something is wrong with her taste buds. I say, "I renounce this physical attack of satan, and command in the name of Jesus that her taste buds heal and function normal and that she tastes again." And glory to God, her creative miracle manifests right then and there and she enjoys the pleasurable taste of food again.

A desperate Mama holds up her little child who cannot walk. She tells me about a spinal injury from an infection, and for four years he does not walk. The artistic compassion overwhelms me for this young child. I hold out my hands to her wee one who also does not respond to people. I say, "Let's go for a walk with Jesus." And suddenly he walks to the wonderment of his mother and the people around.

An old friend reveals to me her life's pain. As she speaks, demonic expressions appear on her face. She is unaware, but I clearly see what manifests before me. With heartfelt words I introduce her to Jesus and give her the invitation to receive Him as Savior. She accepts, prays, and the moment she is born again, she automatically receives her deliverance.

The healing service comes to an end, I minister to everyone in the line. I look to the back to the sound booth and ask the young lady working with the sound if she has a need for healing. Little do I know, she was born with deafness and wears hearing aids. She quickly comes forward. I lay miracle working hands upon her ears. I renounce the spirit of deafness and prophetically create with faith-filled words a new set of hearing ears.

What situation stands before you? What opportunity awaits your creative verbal command? Who comes to your mind right now? Are you being convicted to surrender to the spirit of prophecy, Jesus Himself, and release His power to heal?

Kathy Harmon's Healing Testimony

I was sitting down during the lunch break chatting with one of the out-of-state guests, Kathy Harmon, at a recent healing seminar in Purcellville, Virginia. This woman came with various needs for healing. She began to tell me that she was a nurse and how sometimes her profession can stand in the way of supernatural healing. James 5:16 (AMP) tells us to:

> *Confess your sins to one another [your false steps, your offenses], and pray for one another, that you may be healed and restored. The heartfelt and persistent prayer of a righteous man (believer) can accomplish much [when put into action and made effective by God—it is dynamic and can have tremendous power].*

But despite her human reasoning, Kathy was determined, and she came to the healing seminar anyway, with a need for a healing in her retina. It appeared she had a hole, tear, or detachment taking place in her retina. This caused her great concern as it can lead to blindness. She also had need for the healing of her sinuses.

A week later, Kathy wrote me with excitement to share the good report from the healing seminar. She writes:

> I just wanted to let you know what happened after you prayed and laid hands on my eyes. I went back to the eye specialist. She stated the visceral detachment did not cause any retinal tears or detachment! She asked me to come back for a checkup

in one year…the usual amount of time for a visceral detachment to heal is 3 months or more, mine started about 5 weeks ago and did no further damage after you prayed for me. I was given an extensive eye exam and pronounced to have very good vision. The next morning after you prayed for me I was awakened by a "crackling" noise in my sinuses! It sounded like someone was crumpling up a piece of newspaper, but the sound was in my sinuses. Then suddenly it was like a strong gust went through my sinuses and I could breathe like I never have before!

Imagine what it was like for her to wake up to what she thought was someone crumpling a newspaper near her, only to realize it was the Holy Spirit recreating her sinuses, then feeling a gust of air blow through them, and suddenly being able to breathe freely.

The verse that comes to my spirit immediately after reading this comes from First Corinthians 2:9 that declares, *"Eye has not seen, nor ear heard, nor have entered into the heart of man the things which God has prepared for those who love Him."*

The natural person, the five senses, human reasoning, and medical reports, no matter how brilliant, how accurate, or how sense-filled they may be, none can see and hear into the supernatural realm of God. It takes the eyes and ears of faith to believe when everything else tells us not to.

What an awesome healing testimony this is. Kathy's retina and sinuses all healed at the same time. What part did she play in this wonderful healing? The day before, she participated in an all-day healing seminar. She wasn't just a spectator during this seminar, she engaged in the healing message, latched onto the power of the Holy Spirit, and in doing so she created an atmosphere of faith for her healing within her heart by saturating her being with healing words, which caused the presence of God to infiltrate her domain and release creative healing in her sinuses and retina. All were healed and made whole.

Word of the Lord

THE WORD OF THE LORD FOR YOU TODAY IS, *"My blessings wait for you to speak them into existence. Be bold and courageous, don't hold back. Joy abounds and waits for you to be My expression of the prophetic power that heals. Climb on board, and don't delay. Miracles are on standby, waiting for the word of release."*

Let's pray: *"Dear Holy Spirit, teach me this day how to efficiently swing my sling and release You with full power into every situation that I confront. Show me how to effectively tap into the power of Your grace with unmerited favor beyond measure. In Jesus' name, amen."*

You've learned five ways to release healing with the positive force of your tongue and how even something as simple as pleasant words possess powerful healing properties. You've been made aware of the importance of the present tense of faith, and just how this affects your healing. You've given thought to how David brought Goliath down and even discovered that his five stones were not just any old stones, but grace-activated with divine favor; and in the name of the Lord He won the battle that raged against him, and so can you.

Now, let's turn to the next chapter and study the creative and positive blessing of our words and how these words will help us in the days to come.

Personal Word Checkup

Do I realize that my words dictate the direction of my life? Will I declare the faithfulness of Jehovah Rapha to keep His healing promises to me? Am I willing to produce supernatural healing with the prophetic power of my words? Do I encourage trust with my words to believe for the miraculous? Do I take ownership of sickness and disease with my words, or do I deny them entrance? Do I take advantage of the healing properties of pleasant words? Do I build up or tear down with my words? Am I willing to share God's grace, His unmerited favor with others? Am I challenged to get creative with my words to heal?

Group Discussion

Discuss with your group the five steps to empower the tongue and minister accordingly to the needs that will arise within the group.

Questions for Chapter 4—The Creative and Positive Blessing of Words

1. What do spoken words dictate?

2. List five ways the positive force of the tongue releases healing.

3. What do gracious or pleasant words possess?

4. *Oikodomē* is Greek for which word? What does it mean?

5. How does David activate the power of His words?

6. What does the number five symbolize in the Bible?

7. What does the enemy always have?

8. Does the enemy have the mind of Christ?

9. What are five steps to empower the tongue?

10. What is faith in the last subtitle?

Endnotes

1. Bible Encyclopedia, "Slings and stones"; https://christiananswers .net/dictionary/sling.html; accessed April 5, 2018.

2. BibleStudy.org, "Meaning of Numbers in the Bible"; http://www .biblestudy.org/bibleref/meaning-of-numbers-in-bible/5.html; accessed April 5, 2018.

CHAPTER 5

THE POWER OF LIFE AND DEATH IN THE TONGUE

Your words cause both good and bad things to come to pass in your life. It all depends on what you say. Will you speak life or death over yourself, your loved ones, or your present situation? Your words actually create life or death. Be careful, for what you say will eventually come to pass.

Word of the Lord

THE LORD YOUR GOD WOULD SAY TO YOU THIS DAY, *"Speak life, and continue to speak life. Declare strength in your mortal body. Healing will manifest if you will remain faithful and true to the promise of My Word. My Word gives life to the receiver, and the one who will voice activate My promise is wise and lives. I say to you again, speak life, and continue to speak life."*

The Power of Life and Death in Your Tongue

There is so much confusion within the Body of Christ and so little teaching from the pulpit about the power of life and death in the tongue. The following is a prayer request from a woman suffering from many ailments.

The first time I pray with her the prayer of faith, then she responds again and again, and I can see my words are not accomplishing what they are being sent out to do because she continues to speak death to her body.

She writes again, "I continue to lose my hair and cannot sleep. My eyes get so dry. My whole body is dry. I am losing so much weight too. Can you break all of that off of me so I can live again?"

This time I respond with the following response, "Dear Sister-in-Jesus, you are the one who needs to do this. First of all, stop speaking such negative things over yourself and start to call those things that are not as though they are already recreated and healed in Jesus' name."

She quickly responds again with the all too common response I receive from many seeking healing: "Can you please help me? I do not understand this." Her response is another confirmation of the need within the Body of Christ for in-depth teaching concerning the power of the spoken word and how our tongue possesses the power of life and death. Once God's people catch the revelation of the power of the tongue, physical healing manifests.

Proverbs 18:21

Proverbs 18:21 states, *"Death and life are in the power of the tongue, and those who love it will eat its fruit."* The Amplified Version expounds upon this verse as follows, *"Death and life are in the power of the tongue, and those who love it and indulge it will eat its fruit and bear the consequences of their words."* And the Complete Jewish Bible says it this way, *"The tongue has power over life and death; those who indulge it must eat its fruit."* Whereas the Message Bible plainly states, *"Words kill, words give life; they're either poison or fruit—you choose."*

Hebrew Words and Their Meanings in Proverbs 18:21			
ENGLISH	HEBREW	MEANING	STRONG'S REFERENCE[1]
Death	*maveth*	death (natural or violent), pestilence, ruin	H4194

Hebrew Words and Their Meanings in Proverbs 18:21

English	Hebrew	Meaning	Strong's Reference[1]
Life	*chay*	living, alive, green (of vegetation), flowing, fresh (of water), lively, active (of man), reviving (of the springtime), life, sustenance, maintenance, revival, renewal	H2416
Power	*yad*	hand of, strength and power	H3027
Tongue	*lashown*	language, speaker	H3956
Love	*'ahab*	human appetite for wisdom	H157
Eat	*'akal*	consume or devour	H398
Fruit	*pĕriy*	reward	H6529

To recap Proverbs 18:21 from the English and Hebrew meaning of the words, we understand that death (natural or violent, pestilence, ruin), life (living, alive, green of vegetation, flowing, fresh of water, lively, active of man, reviving of the springtime, life, sustenance, maintenance, revival renewal), power (strength and power are in the hand of the language of the speaker), love (human appetite for wisdom) will eat (consume and devour) the fruit (reward) of their spoken words.

Yes, according to the Good News in Proverbs 18:21, the Holy Spirit teaches us that there is the power of life and death in our tongues. Essentially this means that the condition of our health is in the words we speak. In other words, we have control over our health and lives. With this revelation, let us learn how to speak words of faith that will produce healing, health, and strength into our mortal bodies.

You see, according to God, our words either create or destroy. We can learn to use the power of the spoken word wisely. We need to destroy the work of the enemy, satan, in our lives. We are to renounce sickness, disease, and death attacking our bodies. And then we release the healing power of the Holy Spirit and receive it into sick body parts.

Jesus says in Mark 11:22-24, *"Have faith in God. For assuredly, I say to you, whoever says to this mountain, 'Be removed and be cast into the sea,' and does not doubt in his heart, but believes that those things he says will be done, he will have whatever he says. Therefore I say to you, whatever things you ask when you pray, believe that you receive them, and you will have them."* What were some of the prophetic statements that these people spoke out loud for their healing?

- *"Lord, if You are willing, You can make me clean"* (Luke 5:12).

- *"If only I may touch His garment, I shall be made well"* (Matthew 9:21).

- *"But say the word, and my servant will be healed"* (Luke 7:7).

They worked their faith until their very own words retrieved their health and healing.

A Daughter Activates the Healing Word for Her Mother

I was ministering at a healing service in the State of Virginia, and a woman from another state came to this specific healing service with a special request for her mother's complete healing.

She had watched my interview on Sid Roth's, *It's Supernatural* television program. She ordered my book, *The Healing Creed,* and as soon as it arrived she read the entire book that night to her mother who had suffered from a stroke and had been bedridden with little chance of survival. To her amazement, the very next morning her mother woke up and got out of bed and walked. So the daughter went online and found where I was going to be ministering healing next. She and her mother drove all the way from Chicago, Illinois, down to Purcellville, Virginia, to share this testimony and receive the completion of her mother's healing.

This testimony and other healing testimonies never cease to amaze me about how faith combined with the spoken healing word transform the lives of many individuals.

Healing on Your Tongue

God creates the power of the tongue to release healing, to create miracles, and to build one another up in the faith—not to tear down and discourage one another. Learn to be wise and release healing into your physical body and to others around you.

Bless your body with these healing words from the Scriptures:

* The joy of the Lord is my strength (Nehemiah 8:10).

* Laughter is my medicine (Proverbs 17:22).

* My sleep is sweet (Proverbs 3:24).

* I will run and not grow weary; I will walk and not faint (Isaiah 40:31).

* My faith makes me well (Luke 8:48).

* By His stripes I am healed (Isaiah 53:5).

Be a Giver of Life

With the power of your tongue you can be a giver of life. You can release creative power to open blind eyes, open deaf ears, unmute voices, loose the paralytic, and release healing power to weak and sick body organs and systems. Go deep into the cellular realm with the power of the Spirit and prophetically rearrange dysfunctional DNA. With this prophetic utterance you can send forth resurrection power that raises the dead in spirit, soul, and in the physical body. You can encourage the discouraged and transform depression with joy and laughter. Ponder upon the limitlessness of your verbal expressions and rewrite impossible circumstances into possible ones. Contemplate the glory of God that you can create as you begin to allow the resurrection power of life to roll off your tongue at any given time or place. Be a giver of life.

The Effects of Childhood Polio Healed

The following is a wonderful testimony about a woman who came to the healing conference in Austin, Texas, with multiple issues that caused her great pain. She had contracted polio as a child and it crippled her; then when she was older, she had an accident and the glass from a window cut her leg down to her bone. Another health issue was a torn rotary cuff.

She had heard how she was responsible for her own healing, and that it is her faith that heals her. She received the teaching necessary to know what faith is and how to activate her faith for her healing.

We started with the torn rotary cuff first and I unleashed the power of prophetic healing with my words into her shoulder. She was instantly healed and had full range of movement. And that made her very happy. I then verbally released the healing power down her spine and into her hips. I told her to put her faith into action and do what she was not able to do before. She started to sway her hips back and forth, and within about a minute she was beaming with joy as she was loosed from a lifetime of ill effects from childhood polio.

Then I released the power of the Holy Spirit with my words into her left knee and leg that had been cut through from the glass door accident. She was eager to exercise her faith and the pain and tightness was easing up. I then asked her if she came to the service with someone. And she did so I asked her friend to walk her around the sanctuary, and amazingly she started to walk with ease.

Glory to God, all things are possible to those who believe in the miracle-working power of the Spirit of God. And this woman is a shining example of what happens when people learn what it means to believe, and how to unleash the prophetic healing power of our words and activate the benefits of healing.

Activate the Destructive Force of the Tongue Wisely

There is a time to activate the destructive force of the tongue, but it never is against people. Know who your enemy is. Ephesians 6:12 says, *"For we do not wrestle against flesh and blood, but against principalities, against powers, against the rulers of the darkness of this age, against spiritual hosts of wickedness in the heavenly places."* We are not to verbally destroy people but to bring down the wickedness of the enemy. Like so:

> "In Jesus' name, I renounce the spirit of death and this cancer attacking my body. I command all tumors and cancerous cells to die and disappear." Then you need to move in with the creative, positive force of the tongue. "Now, I release the Spirit of Life, health, and healing throughout my entire body. I command new healthy cells to be recreated. And I declare these new cells are super-smart cells and they outwit every form of cancer there is, in Jesus' name, amen."

How to Give a Proper Faith Response

Okay, you have made the decision to activate faith for your physical healing. But it takes time for you to work out your faith. And you wonder, *How do I respond when people ask me how am I doing?* This response is not as complicated as you have worked it up to be.

According to Scripture, *"by His stripes you were healed"* (Isaiah 53:4-5). It has already happened in the realm of the Spirit, but unbelievers do not understand this. Right? And they cannot because spiritual matters are spiritually discerned; they first need to be born again to understand Kingdom principles. Even many Christians lack the know-how to manifest the Kingdom of God happenings, miracles, into the realm of earth.

So you find yourself back to the original question, *How do I respond when people ask me how am I doing?* Holy Spirit knew you would need instruction about how to respond in faith to activate and keep your healing. He penned through the writings of the apostle Paul in Romans 4:17 the answer, *"(as it is written, 'I have made you a father of many nations'") in the presence of Him whom he believed—God, who gives life to the dead and calls those things which do not exist as though they did.'"*

You are to respond as though the healing has already manifested in your physical body. Like this, *"I am better now, I am stronger than I was yesterday, and in Jesus' name, I am healed."*

Is this lying? No. It is Holy Spirit's radical vocabulary of faith. And this is the only way in which He speaks to create a miracle. He teaches you in Romans 4:17 how to create what you have need of by the power of your spoken words.

And how do your respond when you are asked the same question in regard to a loved one? "In Jesus' name, he or she is healed. Now, we need to line our faith up with (person's name) faith for the complete manifestation of healing. Can we join hands together right now and pray in unity for him or her?"

This type of response is beneficial in several ways. For one, it causes the power of doubt and unbelief to stop, and it releases the healing power of God. This is important to remember.

Moans and Groans

Believe it or not, your moans and groans are a vocabulary onto themselves. Groans like other legible words produce in the physical realm the meaning behind them. In Psalm 5:1 from the New American Standard Bible version, David prays to the Father, *"Give ear to my words, O Lord, consider my groaning."* In the New King James translation it says, *"Consider my meditation."* Whatever you are meditating upon while groaning, these words will produce it. And when you express yourself with moans and groans, others recognize these sounds as expressions of frustration, anger, sadness, disappointment, pain, or agony, and oftentimes they will translate with the power of their words the meaning of your groans. And between your moans and groans and their repeating the translation of your moans and groans, these negative sounds strengthen the sickness, disease, pain, and agony as well, and they actually delay or prevent your healing from manifesting.

In the online Blue Letter Bible Lexicon, the Strong's reference for groaning is H585. The Hebrew word is *'anachah* and it means sighing, groaning (expression of grief or physical distress).[2] The following are a few verses that use this expression and clearly states what groaning in the flesh produces.

- *"I am weary with my groaning; all night I make my bed swim; I drench my couch with my tears"* (Psalm 6:6).

- *"Because of the sound of my groaning my bones cling to my skin"* (Psalm 102:5).

- *"For my life is spent with grief, and my years with sighing; my strength fails because of my iniquity, and my bones waste away"* (Psalm 31:10).

Instead of moaning and groaning as you roll out of bed in the morning, may I suggest two options to transform the negativity of fleshly groaning into health and healing? In place of moaning and groaning in the flesh, moan and groan in the Spirit, pray in your heavenly language, in tongues.

Likewise the Spirit also helps in our weaknesses. For we do not know what we should pray for as we ought, but the Spirit Himself makes intercession for us with groanings which cannot be uttered (Romans 8:26).

Or make a conscious effort and bless instead of curse your day with these words, *"This is the day the Lord has made; I will rejoice and be glad in it"* (see Psalm 118:24). If you will keep at this, eventually you will automatically wake up with this blessing rolling off your tongue.

Laughter

Stop and consider the vocal power of laughter. Your laughter has different meanings and produces different results. The supernatural power of laughter heals and strengthens us. It's God's medicine for us.

- *A merry heart does good, like medicine*, but a broken spirit dries the bones (Proverbs 17:22).

- ...Do not sorrow, for *the joy of the Lord is your strength* (Nehemiah 8:10).

- This is the day the Lord has made; *we will rejoice and be glad in it* (Psalm 118:24).

There is also the sinful side of laughter that ridicules and belittles people. It also mocks and doubts God and His miraculous ways. Let's study this.

When God reveals to Abram that his barren wife, Sara, will give birth to a son, he fell on the ground and laughed with doubt and unbelief:

> *Then Abraham fell on his face and laughed, and said in his heart, "Shall a child be born to a man who is one hundred years old? And shall Sarah, who is ninety years old, bear a child?" And Abraham said to God, "Oh, that Ishmael might live before You!" Then God said: "No, Sarah your wife shall bear you a son, and you shall call his name Isaac; I will establish My covenant with him for an everlasting covenant, and with his descendants after him" (Genesis 17:17-19).*

When Sarah first heard that she was to give birth to a son within a year, she too began to laugh with doubt. But the messengers of God called her on it and she lied to them and denied that she laughed:

And He said, "I will certainly return to you according to the time of life, and behold, Sarah your wife shall have a son." (Sarah was listening in the tent door which was behind him.) Now Abraham and Sarah were old, well advanced in age; and Sarah had passed the age of childbearing. Therefore Sarah laughed within herself, saying, "After I have grown old, shall I have pleasure, my lord being old also?" And the Lord said to Abraham, "Why did Sarah laugh, saying, 'Shall I surely bear a child, since I am old?' Is anything too hard for the Lord? At the appointed time I will return to you, according to the time of life, and Sarah shall have a son." But Sarah denied it, saying, "I did not laugh," for she was afraid. And He said, "No, but you did laugh!" (Genesis 18:10-15).

The beauty in all this is that Sarah judged her God faithful. *"By faith Sarah herself also received strength to conceive seed, and she bore a child when she was past the age, because she judged Him faithful who had promised"* (Hebrews 11:11). And the laughter of doubt and unbelief from many years of sorrow of being labeled the barren woman was restored and transformed into laughter of faith and joy and she gave birth to a son and he was called, Isaac, which means laughter and joy. *"And Sarah said, 'God has made me laugh, and all who hear will laugh with me.' She also said, 'Who would have said to Abraham that Sarah would nurse children? For I have borne him a son in his old age'"* (Genesis 21:6-7).

And Abraham too looked to his God and considered not his physical age or condition, nor the age and physical state of his wife and he received strength and seeded Isaac.

(as it is written, "I have made you a father of many nations") in the presence of Him whom he believed—God, who gives life to the dead and calls those things which do not exist as though they did; who, contrary to hope, in hope believed, so that he became the father of many nations, according to what was spoken, "So shall your descendants be." And not being weak in faith, he did

not consider his own body, already dead (since he was about a hundred years old), and the deadness of Sarah's womb. He did not waver at the promise of God through unbelief, but was strengthened in faith, giving glory to God (Romans 4:17-20).

This elderly couple, who were both past the years of childbearing, took part in the power of laughter of belief to seed and conceive the impossible, the miraculous. And God's prophetic words of healing came to pass.

Activate this vocal gift and laugh to heal, not to nullify God's healing power.

Meditation

Do you speak to yourself? If so, you are not alone or strange. God designed us to do so. It is called meditation and it means to mutter or to speak aloud to yourself. We are not to follow after the world's way of meditation, which is to empty yourself. In fact, this type of meditation is very dangerous, it opens you up to the demonic world and you allow them easy access by letting your spiritual guard down and giving them possession of your being. This is not what God intended. God's form of meditation is that we fill ourselves with the Word of God, and as we ponder upon it, we speak it out loud and let the power of God's Word transform us from the inside to the outside.

This Book of the Law shall not depart from your mouth, but you shall meditate in it day and night, that you may observe to do according to all that is written in it. For then you will make your way prosperous, and then you will have good success (Joshua 1:8).

Four Steps to Godly, Biblical Meditation from Joshua 1:8:

1. Develop the healthy habit of daily Bible study.

2. Ponder the message of the Scriptures you are studying throughout the day.

3. Verbalize these verses out loud repeatedly.

4. Live out the Word; do what it says.

Different Forms of Negative Speech

There are consequences for not choosing our words carefully. Let's check out a few examples and learn to correct our words to activate life-filled results.

Worrying and Fretting

Worrying and fretting about things that probably would never happen but for the wagging of negativity from our mouths. This is evil and sinful behavior, it fills the mind with fear and it gets into the heart and comes out of the mouth with words of doubt and unbelief and produces sickness and death. For example:

- "Mom had breast cancer, I'm afraid I'll have it too."

- "Grandpa suffered from strokes. I'm scared I will too."

- "Both Grandma and Mom suffered many years from high blood pressure. I suppose I will too."

Faith quickly snuffs these negative thoughts out, and in their place speaks out declarations of protection such as, "In Jesus' name, I renounce generational curses. I have been redeemed by the blood of the Lamb. My body is strong and healthy and will remain this way all the days of my life."

Jesus is calling all warriors, not worriers to the front line of faith. Faithful warriors for Jesus are strong in their weapons of faith and will use them skillfully. Whereas a worrier doesn't operate in the realm of faith, but in the arena of doubt and unbelief and cannot be called upon for battle because the worrier's words of worry and fret make them weak in the faith. Which one is pleasing to God? And why do you think this would be?

Chronic Complaining

Is it healthy to "Let off a bit of steam" or to "vent" your negative feelings? According to www.dictionary.com, the definition of complaining is to express dissatisfaction, pain, uneasiness, censure, resentment, or grief and to find fault in someone or something. No wonder why complaining is bad for your health.

When you complain, your body releases the stress hormone cortisol. Cortisol shifts you into fight-or-flight mode, directing oxygen, blood, and energy away from everything but the systems that are essential to immediate survival. One effect of cortisol, for example, is to raise your blood pressure and blood sugar so that you'll be prepared to either escape or defend yourself.

All the extra cortisol released by frequent complaining impairs your immune system and makes you more susceptible to high cholesterol, diabetes, heart disease and obesity. It even makes the brain more vulnerable to strokes.[3]

Again, science confirms what is written in the Word so many, many years ago concerning the power in our words, either they contain life or death. And in the case of chronic complaining they produce death to the speaker, the hearer, and into the situation too.

It is one thing to share a grievance or a legitimate concern, but what's not often okay is the motive of the heart behind these complaints. Beware of an evil critical spirit, not only does it want to destroy your health, but the well-being of all.

Word of the Lord

THE SPIRIT WILLS TO ADMONISH YOU THIS DAY, *to stop your complaining and start the power of praising. Release My presence into the atmosphere and praise the name of the Lord your God. Whining and grumbling does not woo the Spirit of God, but I promise to inhabit the praises of My people. Lift up your voice and praise."*

Learn to break the negative habit to complain, and instead find a creative way to express with a positive flare that includes a suggestion with a reasonable solution to change the situation.

Despairing

When you say that you are in the depths of despair, what are you really declaring over yourself? That you are utterly without hope. Is this what you really want to say? Or is this just another example of careless and negative speech? What does the Bible have to say about this? *"We are* [I am] *hard-pressed on every side, yet not crushed; we are* [I am] *perplexed, but not in despair"* (2 Corinthians 4:8). No matter the situation, as long as you believe, there is always hope.

Speak to Stubborn Mountains

And when you release prayers, words filled with faith, you get His attention; and because His word prophesies that faith can move mountains, so too your words of faith will cause those stubborn mountains of sickness and disease to move away from you as well.

> *He [Jesus] replied, "Because you have so little faith. Truly I tell you, if you have faith as small as a mustard seed, you can say to this mountain, 'Move from here to there,' and it will move. Nothing will be impossible for you"* (Matthew 17:20 NIV).

This means that you have a part to play in your healing. Jesus did His part when He shed His healing blood for you at the whipping post in Isaiah 53:4-5. Now, you are responsible to believe and activate your faith with your words and your actions.

Be brave and bold in the power of the blood, knowing that you possess healing power in your faith-filled words. Learn to pray in faith, speak words that line up with faith, and cause those mountains of sickness and disease to fall for God's glory.

Do You Continually Speak to the Mountain?

Another reader writes and asks, "When believing for healing manifestation, do I continually speak to the mountain or do I just keep thanking God and confess my healing or both?"

This is a great question. It depends upon the way you are speaking. Are you speaking *about* the mountain, which will increase its demonic stronghold over you? Or are you speaking *to* the mountain with the authority of Christ in a way that will cause it to lose its power over you?

Generally speaking, you want to speak with authority to it in such a way that the demonic power behind it clearly understands you will not tolerate this sickness or physical problem anymore. For example, "In Jesus' name, I thank You that I am delivered and healed. My heart is recreated and functions perfectly normal. I will not die, but live and declare the glory of the Lord."

Help—the Mountain Appears to be Getting Bigger and Stronger!

You are doing your part, declaring, decreeing, commanding, and demanding that this mountain of sickness be removed from your midst, but this mountain appears to be getting bigger and stronger. You need advice because you are not sure what is going on with this situation. You want help to heal.

First of all, some mountains are stronger than others. Their foundations run deeper, there are even hidden strongholds that need be unearthed and dealt with. Strongholds such as unforgiveness, pride, shame, and fear just to name a few. Envision these strongholds as individual mountains within the main mountain. These issues have to be dug up, exposed, and dealt with before the main mountain will move. You have to destroy these internal mountains from the inside to the outside. While at the same time, maintain the faith of your words to bring the entire mountain down.

And remember, you will also rip apart the very fiber of satan's pride and deception against you. He is not going to easily release his power grip on you. He is going to resist your efforts against him. You will have to fight to force his deadly jaw and the effects of his lying tongue to let you go in Jesus' name.

Remember, God Is Not the Mountain

It's important to know and remember that God is not the mountain standing in your way, satan is. Therefore, while speaking *to* this mountain, and not *about* the mountain, you do not beg God for your answer. He completed His work at Calvary, and now it is your turn to work His work. If you will prophesy accurately to this mountain, it will move and be cast into the sea. Learn to prophesy healing with accuracy, hit the mark, and cause that mountain to crumble from the inside to the outside—and watch it fall down.

This is not a correct healing confession: "Even though I have symptoms in my body, they can do no permanent damage to my body because I was healed at the Cross"? As long as we confess with our mouths that we have symptoms, by the power of these words we will continue to have them. And if we say that these symptoms can have no permanent damage, we constrain them from producing permanent damage, but still allow them to do some level of damage with these types of confessions. And obviously we want to rid ourselves from symptoms all together so it would be better to select faith statements full of authority and bring all forms of symptoms under submission to the Word of God.

In other words, do not give the symptom room to remain in your body and cause suffering. It's better to speak out, "I take the authority given me by the atoning blood of Christ and I declare that I am free and healed from all symptoms, sickness, and disease that try to attack my body. In the mighty name of Jesus, amen."

Go Ahead, Speak Life

Go ahead, speak life, you've got nothing to lose, and everything to gain. Release the Spirit of Life and free yourself from the law of sin and death (see Romans 8:2.) Speak life into that dead marriage or into that painful relationship between you and your child. Prophesy life into the messenger standing in the pulpit you complain about every Sunday morning. Declare God's healing power into that troubled heart, torn rotary cuff, into those arthritic joints. Loose the creative power of the Spirit into the marrow of your bones. Put a stop to the word curses over yourself and get in line with the Holy Spirit and go ahead, speak life!

Prayer

Father God, I have heard this message that I have the power of life and death in my tongue. I see now that our words make a difference. Teach me your ways. I desire to learn to move with success in all areas of the prophetic. In Jesus' name I pray, amen.

We have studied about the power of life and death in the tongue, how to use these supernatural powers correctly. We've even given thought to different expressions of the tongue such as moans and groans, chronic complaining, and laughter. And how to speak to stubborn mountains and how often we should speak to them. In the following chapter, we will give thoughtful consideration as to whether or not our tongues need healing.

Personal Word Checkup

Am I willing to speak life, and only life no matter how I feel? Will I declare strength to my mortal body no matter the medical report? Will I fashion this supernatural weapon and declare God's healing word over myself and my loved ones? Will I voice activate the Spirit of Life and with my same instrument demolish the work of satan in the situation with the power of my words? Do I know how to give a proper faith response when asked how I am doing? Or what to say when asked about a loved one's health? Do I need to repent of moaning and groaning? Do I use laughter to ridicule or belittle people? Or do I use the supernatural power of laughter to heal and get strong? Do I activate the four steps of godly meditation according to Joshua 1:8? Do I struggle with any of these verbal sins, worrying and fretting, chronic complaining, and despairing? Do I understand how to speak to stubborn mountains? Do I speak to them or about them? Do I treat God as if He is the mountain? Do I, will I take the challenge and speak life no matter what?

Group Discussion

A great topic of discussion is speaking to stubborn mountains. It's even more powerful if you have a couple of people willing to share a stubborn mountain they have been either putting up with or dealing with. And together as a group discuss how to correctly speak to mountains and command them to fall down. Join hands and pray aloud together.

Questions for Chapter 5—The Power of Life and Death in the Tongue

1. The condition of our health is in what?

2. Jesus gave you the responsibility and empowered you with what type of power to accomplish the impossible?

3. What are some of the things God creates the power of the tongue for?

4. Romans 4:17 teaches you how to create what you have need of by what means?

5. What are the four steps to godly, biblical meditation from Joshua 1:8?

6. What can move mountains?

7. Why do you want to speak with authority to the mountain in your life?

8. If we continue to confess that we have symptoms, what will we have?

Endnotes

1. Hebrew word definitions are provided by Strong's Concordance and can be found at Blue Letter Bible: https://www.blueletterbible.org.

2. https://www.blueletterbible.org.

3. Travis Bradberry, "How Complaining Rewires Your Brain for Negativity," September 9, 2016; https://www.entrepreneur.com/article/281734; accessed April 5, 2018.

Chapter 6

Does Your Tongue Need Healing?

Word of the Lord

My Spirit calls to you and says, *"Listen to what you say. Heed the prophetic healing message today. Learn of Me and My ways. Bring your tongue under the submission of My Word and live long, prosper in all your ways. Observe the good that you reap by this spiritual tune-up. Testify of the supernatural adjustment that takes place in the atmosphere around you. Let the power of prophetic healing begin."*

Okay, you've heard the biblical evidence that you possess prophetic and healing power on your tongue. The words you speak make a difference, and whether you like it or not, every word counts. The situation you live in today is created by the words you speak in the past. So what are you going to do?

Most people need a radical healing of their vocabulary. Let's face it, since birth you've been raised in a negative world. And this world doesn't take kindly to a positive response of faith. It goes against the fallen nature of humans. But as a Christian, you are placed in this world to make a difference, not to blend in or to be controlled by it. Jesus says in John 17:14-19:

> *I have given them Your word; and the world has hated them because they are not of the world, just as I am not of the world. I do not pray that You should take them out of the world, but that You should keep them from the evil one. They are not of the world, just as I am not of the world. Sanctify them by Your truth. Your word is truth. As You sent Me into the world, I also have sent them into the world. And for their sakes I sanctify Myself, that they also may be sanctified by the truth.*

The starting point to healing your tongue is to recognize and admit that you need this healing in the first place.

A man struggles to be free from alcoholism. He's angry with his parents who have long since passed. His wife, children, and even the grandchildren get the brunt of his temper. His words are filled with violence and fear. And he wonders why he feels alone.

A woman has been married and divorced several times. The problem is always someone else's fault, she has an angry spirit, she's quick to explode, and every time she is mad, which is often, out of her mouth will come the names of her past husbands. And she's oblivious to the fact that her tongue needs healing.

It's easy to discern that this man and woman have a problem. They both need inner healing so that their tongues can heal and be at peace with God, themselves, the past, and with other people. And without being redundant, the majority of Christians, just like these troubled people, are clueless of the severity of the negativity that they speak.

You cry out in agony, "Oh, my aching back." And someone nearby hears and offers to pray with you for healing. "Well, um…my church doesn't believe in that." Once more, it is your own cursed words laying claim of an aching back, and your confession of doubt and unbelief that have you bound to that horrific back pain.

Maybe your situation is not as severe as the three mentioned, but still people's minds are so bent on the negative side of life that even a simple question such as, "How are you doing?" receives a negative response, "I can't complain." This is meant to be a positive response, but it's not. What you are actually saying is, "At the moment, everything seems to be fine, but check back later and I'll probably have something to gripe about."

Or you simply ask someone's age, "And how old are you?" They share their age, you respond with a positive note, "You look much younger, you appear to be strong and healthy." They respond, "Well, I might look strong and healthy, but I tell you I feel the aches and pains of my age." And before you know it, you are caught in the middle of a negative conversation filled with faithless responses about their weak body that is racked with sickness and pain.

I share these simple examples of common conversations to open your eyes to the depth of negativity so that, if it applies to you, you can examine your own tongue to see if it needs to be healed.

Another way to discern if your tongue needs healing is if you can't handle being in the same conversation with a positive person, you've got a problem. If you're slanderous against someone who tends to almost always give a joyful response, something's wrong. And the negativity of your own words will reap a heap of garbage in every area of your life.

Personally, I believe because God's Words are positive and life-changing, that for us, as His disciples, negativity should have the same effect on us as the sound of nails scratching chalkboard. And we ought to cringe every time we hear degrading word curses flow from our own mouths.

Common Negative Word Curses

Negativity can be so subtle that it can often go unnoticed—especially when everyone else around you is just as negative as you are. So to shed some light on this matter, we are going to review a list of common negative word curses that God's people speak against their own bodies and situations daily that affect their health and well-being.

- My pain.

- My cancer.

- My diabetes.

- I am sick and tired.

- I always get sick during flu season.

- I'm sick to death of this situation.

- I'm sick of hearing this.

- This will be the death of me yet.

- Drop dead!

- I'm losing my mind.

- I'm more confused now then I have ever been.

- I can't remember a thing.

- I can't think.

- I'll never figure this out.

- You'll never understand.

- You're a bunch of dead heads.

- This kid is going to drive me insane.

- This burger will give me a heart attack.

- I can't hear.

- I can't see a thing.

- I'm blind as a bat.

- I can't see past the end of my nose.

- I'm poor.

- Nothing ever works out.

- I never win.

- Some days are unbearable.

- Nothing good ever happens to me.

- God doesn't listen to me.

- I pray and nothing changes.

- Healing doesn't work.

- Healing isn't for today.

The plain and simple truth is this—as long as you continue to speak these types of negative curses, you will not be able to attain all that God has designed for you, including a healed body. It works like this, a husband criticizes his wife over and over until she shuts down and no longer responds to him, or responds to him in a negative manner. The physical body responds the same way to your negative word curses, it shuts down and body parts respond negatively and deteriorate and die. It takes a radical sanctification of the Holy Spirit for your tongue to be healed and your body to be made whole again.

I Can't

After a healing seminar a couple comes to me with a few questions, and the quiet, reserved husband tells me, "I hear what you say, but I don't know why I just can't speak these things out loud." I answer him and remind him of the power of life and death in our tongues and that he must verbalize his authority for the sake of his wife's health. He understands and agrees to do so.

While personally ministering to someone else who was given just a few weeks to live, I encourage her in the faith and look for a creative way for her to take a stance against the spirit of death. Something that she can do and have a visual every time she thinks about this negative report. We walk over to the door, I open it and ask her to tell the spirit of death to leave. It is not welcome in her home. She looks at me and says, "I can't do that. Someone might hear me." I respond to her refusal and say, "But no one else is here." She says, "There might be children playing outside in the neighborhood." I walk out the door to take a look and say, "There isn't anyone outside, but us."

"I can't" is a negative phrase; and when we use it, we need to clarify what we really want to say. Either we are telling someone that we do not know how to do something, or that we refuse to say or do something. If we do not know how to do something, then we need to ask for help. And remind ourselves that with God, *"I can do all things through Christ who strengthens me"* (Philippians 4:13). I can learn to use the prophetic healing power of my words. I can exercise my God-given authority and demand the spirit of death to leave me and my home.

If it's the later and we refuse to say or do something, we need to check the motives of our heart and see if our refusal lines up with God's Word, it may or it may not. If it aligns itself with the Bible, then say so. Don't make people try to guess where you stand on an issue. Use your gift of words and tell them why. If your refusal doesn't line up with biblical teaching, then you need to do some soul searching with God and repent.

Words Can Hurt Others and Grieve the Holy Spirit

I believe the use of negative words that cause people to feel small or inferior and less than they are is sinful and grieves the Spirit of God. What we say and how we say it can change a life forever, and not always for the best. We need to choose words that please the Father and give life to others.

Yes, people disappoint us and we disappoint others, but even still we need to exercise grace toward one another and choose words that lead to unity, repentance, and forgiveness. When we feel frustrated, we need to be especially careful to hold our tongues and make sure that our words do not offend. Let's learn to develop our vocabulary to the point that we can express our thoughts and feelings in such a way that we do not devalue or embarrass each other.

A brother offended is harder to win over than a fortified city, and contentions [separating families] are like the bars of a castle (Proverbs 18:19 AMP).

Understand this, my beloved brothers and sisters. Let everyone be quick to hear [be a careful, thoughtful listener], slow to speak [a speaker of carefully chosen words and], slow to anger [patient, reflective, forgiving]; for the [resentful, deep-seated] anger of man does not produce the righteousness of God [that standard of behavior which He requires from us] (James 1:19-20 AMP).

If I speak with the tongues of men and of angels, but have not love [for others growing out of God's love for me], then I have become only a noisy gong or a clanging cymbal [just an annoying distraction] (1 Corinthians 13:1 AMP).

Cussing

You may or may not be surprised at how many Christians cuss nowadays, especially Christian women. You know what I'm talking about—you hear it. You accidently stub your toe and instead of letting out a big "Ouch, that hurts!" nasty cuss words come flying out of some people's mouths. The world defends using cuss words. They claim it actually helps to alleviate pain, but it does not. It only makes them feel better for the moment about the pain they are already experiencing. When you are upset, a good brisk walk releases endorphins and is a much healthier thing to do.

Is cussing okay for Christians to do? No, it's not all right. It's lowering the bar of our moral behavior to that of the world's standards. Remember, we are called by God to make a difference in this world, not to conform to its wickedness.

The emotions that thrust cuss words into the airways are negative in nature—anger, bitterness, aggression, disrespect, frustration, rebellion, and even hate. Just these seven emotions alone prove that Christians should not cuss. We are to live our lives, including our speech, by the nine fruits of the Spirit listed in Galatians 5:22-23, *"But the fruit of the Spirit is love, joy, peace, longsuffering, kindness, goodness, faithfulness, gentleness, self-control. Against such there is no law."*

I remember back in 1979 when I became a brand-new believer. There was a young man my husband had known from his high school days. He was born again a little longer than we were, but his speech was not renewed as of yet. He was sitting in the front row of a large auditorium praising Jesus because he was so amazed my husband was now a Christian, but his vocabulary was so foul that I still remember him. I never saw this man again, but it's interesting that so many years later I can so vividly recall his foul mouth. Your words make an impact, and they reveal the condition of your heart.

And this brings me to today, I am appalled at the use of the "f bomb" and its frequent use in everyday conversations and products such as Christmas wrapping paper, baby announcements, coffee cups, and the like. Christian, you are not to have anything to do with these types of products with this word. It's just plain filth.

Ephesians 4:29 (NIV) warns us about unwholesome talk, *"Do not let any unwholesome talk come out of your mouths, but only what is helpful for building others up according to their needs, that it may benefit those who listen."* Cussing is unwholesome talk and it does not build up or benefit those who use it or those who have to listen to you when you choose to use it.

Word of the Lord

THUS SAYETH THE LORD, *"It is not My will that My people who are called by My name align themselves with the camp of the enemy and attack and defeat one another with evil word curses. I place a high call on you to lift one another up, bless and encourage the other with the power of My words. Give life to all those around you and prophesy what they have need of."*

The Effects of Ungodly

The other day after reading the news that was filled with hate, murder, massacre, child abuse, and sexual sins, I had to literally go on a three-day fast to heal my soul of the ungodliness of it all. And you may need to do this as well just to break off the power behind the griminess of the world's words. Are we to bury our heads in the sand like ostriches? No, but we are to wisely choose what media we put before our eyes.

> *As cold water to a weary soul, so is good news from a far country* (Proverbs 25:25).

Words Are Purified

Let's examine the prophetic sanctification process of the tongue.

In the Book of Isaiah, we read how the prophet Isaiah, who would be given prophetic words to speak to the people, had to have his words purified by the Spirit of God. It says in chapter 6, starting with verse 5 and continuing through verse 7:

> *So I said: "Woe is me, for I am undone! Because I am a man of unclean lips, and I dwell in the midst of a people of unclean lips; for my eyes have seen the King, the Lord of hosts." Then one of the seraphim flew to me, having in his hand a live coal which he had taken with the tongs from the altar. And he touched my mouth with it, and said: "Behold, this has touched your lips; your iniquity is taken away, and your sin purged."*

In this verse we read how Isaiah, the prophet and seer, sees into the supernatural realm in a vision. He sees the throne room of God and he becomes unglued in the presence of the Lord and has a revelatory moment and realizes that he and those he is called to prophesy to are defiled in their speech. He understands that his lips need to be sanctified by the Lord. His vocabulary needs forgiveness.

And like this prophet, we too have to come to the realization that our tongues are full of wickedness and can produce great evil, even our words of doubt and unbelief are sinful and need to be forgiven. We need to repent from a negative form of vocabulary that goes against the promises of God so our words can be sanctified and we can prophesy healing, health, and the miraculous as the Spirit wills.

Yes, this portion of Scripture is dealing with the prophet Isaiah, but according to Acts 2:17-21, in these last days we can all move in the realm of the prophetic—and the prophetic starts with the law of the spoken word. It takes words of faith spoken out loud to activate prophetic signs and wonders. And so yes, what happens with Isaiah the prophet pertains to us as well. We need our mouths, lips, tongues, and our words to be touched by the Spirit of God so that our physical bodies and circumstances can be healed and transformed for the glory of the Lord.

> *In the last days, God says, I will pour out my Spirit on all people. Your sons and daughters will prophesy, your young men will see visions, your old men will dream dreams. Even on my servants, both men and women, I will pour out my Spirit in those days, and they will prophesy. I will show wonders in the heavens above and signs on the earth below, blood and fire and billows of smoke. The sun will be turned to darkness and the moon to blood before the coming of the great and glorious day of the Lord. And everyone who calls on the name of the Lord will be saved* (Acts 2:17-21 NIV).

Catch the Little Foxes

Before we tackle the big-ticket items that need serious prophetic healing, we are going to focus for a little while on the common, day-to-day, seemingly harmless phrases that we speak over ourselves that often cause us a lot of trouble. And they may even be the source of a much bigger problem. The Song of Solomon 2:15 advises us to *"Catch us the foxes, the little foxes that spoil the vines, for our vines have tender grapes."* Foxes are considered to be destructive animals that can destroy valuable vineyards. Spiritually speaking about the prophetic and healing power of our words, the little foxes are our everyday words we use that can harm us. And we need to go on a fox hunt and catch them before they destroy us.

Here's a prime example of a little fox spoiling the vine: "Failure is not an option." It's a true statement, but it produces fear about possible failure. Whereas, "Success is the only option" changes the focus from failure to success. And it actually transforms the way someone thinks, speaks, and works these words to fruition.

Transform Negative Everyday Phrases into Positive Statements	
Negative Phrase	*Positive Phrase*
I am so sick and tired of...	I need to take a break to refresh.
I'll never figure this out.	This may be challenging, but I have the mind of Christ.
You'll never understand.	I need you to sit down and listen to what I have to say.
I can't see past the end of my nose.	Oops! I missed that. I'll pay closer attention next time.
I have such bad luck.	I am blessed with the favor of God.
I'm just poor.	My God shall supply my every need.
This food will give me a heart attack.	Perhaps, I should eat healthier.
I always catch the flu.	I need to strengthen my immune system to stay healthier.
I can't hear a thing.	There's a lot of noise here, can you speak louder?
I can't see anything.	I need to move to get a better view.
This kid is going to drive me insane.	I need to set boundaries with my child.

Transform Negative Everyday Phrases into Positive Statements	
Negative Phrase	*Positive Phrase*
My body is falling apart.	I think I need to start exercising to strengthen my body.

We carelessly use negative phrases that do us physical harm. With just this short list of negative phrases, we curse ourselves with poverty, misunderstandings, communication problems, sickness, bad vision, poor hearing, heart attacks, a weak body, insanity, and even premature death. This is why we need to put some thought into what we really do want to say. There is a way to say what we mean without cursing ourselves or causing damage to others. For this reason I added positive alternatives to the list above to help us communicate our thoughts in a healthier manner.

Ask the Right Questions

When things go wrong we often want to blame others, even God, for things that we are responsible for. Instead of using our words to blame others, we need to mature in the faith and use our words efficiently and ask ourselves the right questions, like Jesus would ask troubled people with whom He came into contact.

Jesus asked many questions. The following is a list of seven from the New International Version of the Bible. Read and think about these questions. How do you respond to Him? Do you mainly respond with faith, or do your answers reveal a problem with negativity on your tongue? Do you see the need for the healing of your tongue in this area?

1. Can any one of you by worrying add a single hour to your life? (Matthew 6:27)

2. Do you believe that I am able to do this? (Matthew 9:28)

3. Why did you doubt? (Matthew 14:31)

4. What do you want me to do for you? (Matthew 20:32)

5. Why are you thinking these things? (Mark 2:8)

6. Where is your faith? (Luke 8:25)

7. What do you want? (John 1:38)

Using our words in a wiser manner to ask poignant questions is far more effective than blaming and accusing others.

Corrupt Communication

We have studied extensively throughout this work about the ill effects of corrupt communication such as cussing, gossiping, lying, complaining, and more. Do you need to make any adjustments in the way you express yourself to others, or to God?

Do Your Words Defile Your Body?

We have discovered that the words we say affect our body. Every word counts, and each one either produces life or death. As you have pondered this message, what have you been prophesying over yourself? Have you been creating life or death in your physical body?

You Can Do This Too

I tell you the truth, when I say that I am not able to count the number of people who have said to me, "I wish I could do what you do." And my response to them has always been the same, as it is to you today, "You can."

I share with you these foundational truths that will take that mediocre Christian walk of yours and transform it into something bigger than you could ever imagine. Think about all the good you can do in the name of your Lord if you will take this message to heart and put it into practice. Not only will you and your family heal in spirit, soul, and in physical body, but those around you will heal too.

You won't have to look far and long for someone to minister to, they will come to you. You will have more opportunity to minister than you have time for. There are sick and dying people all around you. And they need you to rise to the occasion and prophesy healing into their pain-ridden bodies for the glory of the Lord.

Rate Your Tongue with These Checklists

The usage of words is a very broad subject, and I thought it would be beneficial to have checklists to help pinpoint areas in your vocabulary that need improvement. Use the following checklists and answer yes or no to the following questions. Yes = 1 Point.

		Checklist 1
YES	NO	
		Do I refrain from saying something because either it will cause harm, or it is just plain wrong to say?
		Am I able to control my tongue, especially when under pressure or when my body is racked with physical pain and suffering?
		Do I take a moment to think before I speak, so that I can respond to a situation, rather than just react negatively?
		Do I command the devil to be silent?
		Does my tongue promote health and healing?
		Instead of arguing, do I exercise patience and control and explain to those with different beliefs why I believe in the power of the Holy Spirit to heal?
		Do I declare praise to God for His faithfulness to keep His promise to heal?
		Do I produce supernatural healing with the power of my prophetic words?
		Do I encourage others to trust God for their miracles?

YES	NO	
		Do I deny ownership of sickness and disease by the power of the blood?
		Do I guard my body from illness by prohibiting it entrance with my words?
		Are my words gracious and pleasant and filled with healing properties?
		Do I speak to God in the presence tense of *Now Faith*?
		Do I surrender to the spirit of prophecy, Jesus Himself, and release His power to heal?
		Do I speak words of faith that produce healing, health, and strength into body?
		Do I know and confess the healing Scriptures over myself and family?
		Am I a giver of life with my words?
		Do I activate the destructive force of the tongue with wisdom?
		Do I know how to give a proper faith response?
		Do I speak words of faith over stubborn mountains and command them to move in Jesus' name?

Total number of points for Checklist 1 _____.

	Checklist 2	
YES	NO	
		Do I speak before I think and just blurt out whatever comes to mind?
		Am I constantly in trouble because I say things I shouldn't?
		Do I often find myself conversing with the devil?

		Do I have loose lips that sink shiploads of people from trusting God for their miracles?
		Do I intentionally or unintentionally speak word curses over people?
		Do I curse my brothers and sisters in the Lord who believe differently than I do?
		Do I bless God in congregational worship and then ignorantly curse Him to others with words of unbelief about His ability to heal?
		Do I repeatedly hurt others with abusive speech?
		Do I take the passive route and choose to say nothing and sit back and watch the enemy ravage the life of another?
		Do I activate the power of the name of a disease or that I am healed by the blood of Jesus?
		Do I participate in society's hate speech or in the power of God's love?
		With the poisonous use of words of doubt and unbelief, do I hinder ministering angels and release the destructive powers of demons?
		Do I give strength to disease with moans and groans?
		Do I produce negative results by the sin of worrying and fretting?
		Am I a chronic complainer?
		Do I speak negative word curses that hurt me and others?
		Even though I know better, do I still refuse to speak words of faith?
		Do I cause people to feel less than God intended by speaking negative words over them?
		Do I justify my right to cuss?

		Am I polluting my spirit with a constant barrage of negative news?
Total Number of Points for Checklist 2 _____		

Which checklist did you score higher on? If you scored higher on Checklist 1, then the prophetic and healing power of your words is stronger than weaker. If you scored higher on Checklist 2, then you have your work cut out for you and need to improve the use of the prophetic and healing power of your words to make them work for you.

Test Score for Checklist 1

If you score between the numbers 1-6, this means your tongue needs healing. But don't be discouraged, the positive is that you recognize your fault and this is the beginning step to the much-needed healing of your tongue.

If your score is between the numbers 7-12, your use of words needs improvement. But praise God, He never intends us to do this on our own. He gives us His Helper—Holy Spirit—to lead us and guide us into all truth.

A score between the numbers 13-17 signifies you are well on your way to creating life and miracles, and probably are already, but perhaps sporadically. Don't stop now, go for the prize—a tongue that is well-pleasing to the Father.

If you can judge your words with a number range from 18-20 your daily vocabulary is very positive and life-giving. Well done! Keep up the good work, and don't grow weary in well doing. The Lord needs the maturity of the prophetic and healing power of your words to do His bidding—win the lost for God's glory.

Test Score for Checklist 2

If you score between the numbers 1-6, this means you need some improvement; and if you will pay closer attention to what comes out of your mouth, especially negativity, you will get to where you want to be quickly.

If your score is between the numbers 7-12, your choice of words is not where it should be, but with God's help you can do better. Don't get discouraged, God's not. The positive is that you are willing to move forward and learn how to speak the way He created you to speak.

A score between the numbers 13-20, signifies that you have quite a bit of work ahead of you. Get into the Word of God and allow it to transform your mind. What you put into your spirit will come out of your mouth. And remember, with God all things are possible.

Part One has been somewhat painful, and sometimes a harsh reality of the misuse of the gift of language, but I believe this study is life-changing. The confrontation of the sins of the tongue is absolutely necessary in order to move into the supernatural realm of prophetic healing. And this is where God desires and expects His people to be. As we come to grips with the power we have within our words, we will learn to appropriate this supernatural gift and not only bless ourselves and our families, but all those we come in contact with. In reality, the repentance and transformation of our tongues will be a major move of the Spirit to usher us into the realm of the bride who is ready to meet her Groom—Jesus, in these last days.

In Part Two, we will wield the supernatural weapon of the spoken word and start to put what we have learned thus far into practice with practical and powerful elements of faith such as binding and loosing, confessions, decrees, and declarations of faith. We will sharpen our swords of the Spirit in the power of our spiritual languages and words of knowledge and so much more. Get ready as you turn the page to transform the prophetic and healing power of your words today.

Closing Prayer of Repentance after Studying Part One

Dear Holy Spirit,

After all these years, the revelation of the power of my words has been revealed to me. I come before You on bended knee and seek You for forgiveness for such poor usage of my words. Sometimes my ill use of words has been out of sheer ignorance, while other times I knew exactly what I was saying and that the messages were sinful and damaging to the receiver. And in those instances, Your Spirit was speaking to my spirit, convicting me, but I was just willfully stubborn and rebellious toward You.

My tongue has been unruly and ungodly to say the least. With deep sorrow and regret I understand the havoc my words have created in my life, my marriage, the lives of my children, my friendships, my church, and on the job. I have offended so many, starting with You, Lord, and my spouse, my kids, my pastor, my boss, my fellow coworkers, and even my next-door neighbors.

My poor choice of words has caused sickness, disease, and pain to reign in my body, they have hindered Your supernatural reply and supply to every area imaginable. I have not been a good steward with my words. I have not been faithful to pray in my natural or spiritual languages. I have often brought disgrace upon Your most holy name by taking it in vain. With the negative use of my own words I have discouraged others from trusting and believing in Your promises of hope and life. I have often whined and complained, murmured and gossiped. I have lied and exaggerated, I have crossed the boundaries and insulted and ridiculed others I thought were lesser than myself. I have allowed the unruliness of my tongue to control my life instead of submitting to You and surrendering my words to Your will.

Forgive me for all the time I wasted, for all the grief, pain, and ungodliness my words have caused. With Your guidance, I humbly dare to hit the restart button and begin afresh and anew for Your purpose and glory.

I desire now, more than ever to turn the page and start over in the area of my speech. I desire to be an instrument of honor and praise for Your glory, a wise warrior that is skillful with the sword of the Spirit, piercing the darkness with the light of Your Word. Overcoming evil with good, hate with Your love, sickness with healing, bewilderment with the prophetic wisdom of Your Spirit.

I know that I know this cannot be accomplished by my might or strength, but only by the power of Your Spirit, and I make this quality decision this day to be willing, teachable, and pliable to Your guidance. Where You lead I will follow, what you say I will do. I surrender my tongue to You this day, and I prayerfully desire to comply with Psalm 19:14 and ask for Your assistance that, "The words of my mouth and the meditation of my heart be acceptable in Your sight, O Lord my strength and my Redeemer." In Jesus' name, I pray, amen.

Personal Word Checkup

Since what I live in today is created by the words I speak in the past, "What am I going to do?" Will I humble myself and remain pliable for the Holy Spirit to instruct? Or will I act stiff-necked and rebellious and turn a deaf ear to His teachings about the power of my words? Am I willing to seek help if I do not know how to do something? Or do I just simply rebel against God and say, "I can't." Am I guilty of using negative words that make people feel less than God intended? Should I go on a fast to cleanse myself from the griminess of the world's misuse of words? Do my words need a touch from the Holy Spirit? Am I aware of the little word foxes that spoil the vine in my life? Am I willing to learn how to transform negative phrases into positive ones? Will I start to ask myself the right questions when things go wrong? Or will I continue to blame God and others instead?

Group Discussion

Together read through the list of negative phrases and what each one will produce. Feel free to add more phrases to this discussion. The point is to make the group members aware of the negative word phrases and the physical curses they speak over their bodies. And for each additional negative word curse that is added to the list, transform it to a positive phrase. And discuss with the participants in your group the possibility of fasting and praying for three days to cleanse yourselves from the negative force your words have worked against you.

Questions for Chapter 6—Does My Tongue Need Healing?

1. What do most people need in regard to their vocabulary?

2. What doesn't this world take kindly to?

3. According to the words of Jesus in John 17:14-19, why are Christians placed in this world?

4. What is the starting point to heal your tongue?

5. What will the negativity of your own words reap?

6. What does prophet Isaiah realize during a revelatory moment?

7. What do we need to do when we realize that our tongues are full of negativity and wickedness?

PART TWO

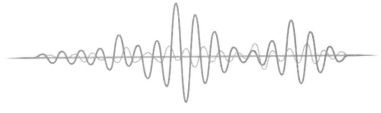

WIELD THE SWORD OF THE SPIRIT

CHAPTER 7

SHARPEN YOUR SPIRITUAL USE OF WORDS

You want to be effective in the Kingdom of God. But how do you fight things that you cannot see? What is the sword of the Spirit? And why has God given this to you?

Word of the Lord

THE SPIRIT OF THE LORD WOULD SAY TO YOU, *"If you are willing, I will lead you into the deep truths, the secret keys found throughout My Word. These secret keys will loose the answers that have been reserved just for you. Open up My Word and learn from Me."*

Ephesians 6:12 informs us that we are in a battle on this earth, and it is not a physical battle of people against other people, but a spiritual battle against demonic forces. It says, *"For we wrestle not against flesh and blood, but against principalities, against powers, against the rulers of the darkness of this age, against spiritual hosts of wickedness in the heavenly places."* And we cannot fight the things of the spirit in the strength of the flesh, it has to be done with the supernatural weaponry that God has equipped His people with.

A relevant instance is dealing with deliverance. I have had to stop well-meaning people from physically harming the demon possessed individual because they have not been properly taught how to deal with spiritual matters. You cannot force a demon to leave with fists or sticks. And once you enter into this type of behavior, you've lost the battle. Demons are in the business of torment, and they encourage you to beat away on the already tormented individual. Stop. Learn to fight the good fight of faith with shining success.

The Bible is clear that we will go through difficulties on this earth. Look at what Jesus says in John 16:33, *"These things I have spoken to you, that in Me you may have peace. In the world you will have tribulation; but be of good cheer, I have overcome the world."* Jesus' words are clear, here in this world you will have tribulation, meaning difficult times. And the spiritual battle is not always easy to discern as the situation mentioned with a demoniac. But whether obvious or not, Jesus desires us to live in His victory when these battles come. And He has given us the weapons to overthrow the real enemy.

How do we live in His victory against the wiles of the devil? God gives us a supernatural weapon called the Sword of the Spirit, His Holy Word. And He expects us to use it. Revelation 12:11 says, *"And they overcame him by the blood of the Lamb and by the word of their testimony...."* Our spiritual weapons in this verse to overcome are the redemptive blood of Jesus, and by the word of our testimony. And when we align the word of our testimony with God's Word, the Bible, the evil strategies of the devil are hindered. And when worked to the fullest supernatural potential, it overpowers his wickedness and our victories manifest in the physical realm. It's imperative for us, God's people, to learn how to wield our supernatural swords, and we will train for this very thing in this chapter, and likewise, sharpen the spiritual power of our words.

In order to wield your sword effectively, you need to train to rightly handle the Word of God. Hebrews 4:12 describes God's Word as *"living and powerful, and sharper than any two-edged sword, piercing even to the division of soul and spirit, and of joints and marrow, and is a discerner of the thoughts and intents of the heart."* And even before the training can begin, you need to take the time and first sharpen your supernatural blade.

Most Christians don't give thought to sharpening their spiritual sword until this vital weapon is no longer sharp. And the truth of the matter is that nothing impacts the longevity of your sword, or its daily performance more than regular sharpening and maintenance. A dull sword in the Kingdom is dangerous and ineffective. Daily sharpening and maintenance is necessary, and the end result is a more efficient and safer blade in the daily battles of life.

What happens if your sword is dull? Let's look at this in the natural. My family is staying at the beach this week and eating fresh fish daily from the ocean. But in order for my husband to prepare the fish for the grill, he has to have a real sharp edge on the blade of his knife, otherwise he feels frustrated because he knows he can do a better job, and the fish is difficult to slice and turns out to be a big mess. It's the same way in the spiritual battles of our lives as well. If our spiritual blades are dull, they cannot thoroughly gut out the enemy; therefore, parts of his wickedness remain in the situation, like a root of bitterness in a relationship, or cancer in the body.

You want complete healing, not partial healing. You desire eternal restoration, not a temporal fix. And in order for your healing and deliverance to be complete, with nothing lacking, your blade needs to be razor-sharp. You simply cannot destroy the works of satan with a dull blade.

To sharpen a blade, you take a honing stone and slide the blade back and forth at an angle until the edge of the blade is sharp. Or you can take two blades and sharpen them against one another. The second way causes the blades to become extremely sharp and efficient to cut with.

We can look at it this way, we first form a sharp edge on our spiritual sword, the prophetic and healing power of our words, by sharpening them upon the honing stone, the all-powerful Holy Scriptures. Then as we mature in the faith, we continue to sharpen our supernatural skills of the use of the Word with another mature believer to train and challenge, rebuke and edify one another with the Scriptures. Proverbs 27:17 gives us a visual picture of this, *"As iron sharpens iron, so a man sharpens the countenance of his friend."*

This process is easier than you think: to start, open up your Bible, read and study it and do what it says to do. To keep the edge of your blade sharp, you need to be consistent, be faithful, spend time in the Word alone with God, and sharpen your skills with others.

Another point of interest is that you need to lubricate the honing stone with water or oil. I love this fact because I believe if you just have the Word you become religious and dry in your spirit. So you need the flow of the Holy Spirit activated in your life with the Word.

And in my study about how to sharpen a blade I also find that instructions speak about the stone being on a flat service. This brings to my mind the importance to make sure there is a balance between the Word and the Holy Spirit. If we have all Holy Spirit and no Word, we become unbalanced and easily led astray. You must be level, balanced in the Word and in the Spirit.

In the beginning, Adam and Eve were sharp in the Spirit, but they dulled themselves by sin. And this is how our spiritual weaponry loses its sharp edge and effectiveness to pierce the darkness. Not taking the time to meditate upon the Scriptures is a sin and dulls your blade quickly. Take a moment and ponder upon this for a moment. Ask yourself, *Is my sword losing its edge? What's the main reason for this? Am I willing to get into the Holy Scriptures and sharpen my sword?*

Hold Up Your Sword for the Duration of the Entire Battle

What will happen if you are in the midst of a battle on the frontline and reach the point of weariness and drop your sword? Your enemy will gain the upper edge and win. In the middle of a fierce fight, you cannot afford to lay down your sword, you have to remain strong and fight your enemy to the finish with your already sharpened sword. And in reality, it is Jesus' finished work on the cross that you are activating with your sword.

Connect with God by Using His Word

We connect with God's Spirit when we use His words and prophesy over ourselves, confess His promises, decree and declare things in the spirit realm, and release prayers of faith filled with praise and thanksgiving. We capture His attention when we verbally activate His Word with our faith.

When you feel weak and tempted to give up, prophesy over yourself, *His grace is sufficient for me* (see 2 Corinthians 12:9).

While you face a difficult situation, start to transform the way you perceive your ability to handle it and confess, *I can do all things through Christ who strengthens me* (see Philippians 4:13).

If you receive a bad medical report from a physician, decree healing into your body with God's healing report:

> *Surely He has borne our griefs and carried our sorrows; yet we esteemed Him stricken, smitten by God, and afflicted. But He was wounded for our transgressions, He was bruised for our iniquities; the chastisement for our peace was upon Him, and by His stripes we are healed* (Isaiah 53:4-5).

If you are being tormented by fear, wield the Word of God and declare, *For God has not given me a spirit of fear, but of power and of love and of a sound mind* (see 2 Timothy 1:7).

The most effective way to pray is to pray using God's Word. Use the Bible as your guide and pray in faith over yourself and your loved ones and allow the power of the spoken words of God to heal and make you whole in Jesus' name. I have discovered that wielding God's Words bring results.

Use the keys of the Kingdom and bind satan and his wicked plots against you and loose the desired results and see your miracles manifest.

This is how to wield the Sword of the Spirit, the weapon of the Word: lay hold of it, not just one time, but daily, and speak it out as often as often as you need, and then you actually live what it says.

Whether you use the elements of faith to bind and loose, confess faith for healing, declare or decree, prophesy, or pray in faith, make sure to use the Word of God. Utilize His words and release the prophetic and healing power of the tongue.

Access the Different Powers of His Names

Like words or phrases, names too have meanings and power behind them to produce. Back in the day, a person's name revealed important character traits, so too do the names of God reveal vital character traits about Him. And we should strive to learn the many different names of Yeshua and access these different powers of His names. Let's look up some of His names in the Scriptures and see what they mean.

When we lead someone in a prayer of salvation we lead them to Jesus—*The Savior*. *"For God so loved the world that He gave His only begotten Son, that whoever believes in Him should not perish but have everlasting life"* (John 3:16).

Praying for loved ones to come to know Jesus as their Savior, pray for *The Revealer*—Jesus—to make Himself and the Father known to them. *"All things have been delivered to Me by My Father, and no one knows the Son except the Father. Nor does anyone know the Father except the Son, and the one to whom the Son wills to reveal Him"* (Matthew 11:27).

Jehovah Rapha means *the Lord who heals you* (see Exodus 15:26). When you use this name of the Lord, you are calling to the healing power of the Lord. In other words, you are spiritually accessing the power of the Lord to heal.

Jesus refers to Himself, directly or indirectly as a physician. And the *Great Physician* possesses the power to heal in spirit, soul, and in the physical body. Jesus answered and said to them, *"Those who are well have no need of a physician, but those who are sick"* (Luke 5:31). And He endowed you with this tremendous ability to heal in His name, see Mark 16:14-16.

In Luke 9:11, we see Jesus as *The Healer*. *"But when the multitudes knew it, they followed Him; and He received them and spoke to them about the kingdom of God, and healed those who had need of healing."* There are many healers and methods of healing—all lesser of course. So we need to make sure to follow the Healer of all healers—Yeshua.

When in need of restoration of your mind and emotions, dial up the power that restores and as you call upon your *Restorer*. *"He restores my soul; He leads me in the paths of righteousness for His name's sake"* (Psalm 23:3).

When someone or something dies prematurely, call upon *The Resurrection and The Life* of Christ and raise the dead in His name and for His glory. *"I am the resurrection and the life. He who believes in Me, though he may die, he shall live"* (John 11:25). Romans 8:11 declares, *"But if the Spirit of Him who raised Jesus from the dead dwells in you, He who raised Christ from the dead will also give life to your mortal bodies through His Spirit who dwells in you."*

For deliverance, bind demons of oppressions and possessions and demons of addictions by loosing the power of Jesus—*The Deliverer*—into the situation, *"He has sent me...to proclaim liberty to the captives...to set at liberty those who are oppressed"* (Luke 4:18-21). Along with the power of the Deliverer of all deliverers call for *The Truth*, *"And you shall know the truth, and the truth shall make you free"* (John 8:32).

When you have lost your way spiritually, but also naturally, call forth *God's compass*—His Son, Jesus, *"The way, the truth, and the life"* (John 14:6). He will lead you back to the Father and His ways.

Is your life in turmoil? Reach out and activate your *peace*—Jesus Christ. *"He Himself is our peace..."* (Ephesians 2:14). *"Be anxious for nothing, but in everything by prayer and supplication, with thanksgiving, let your requests be made known to God; and the peace of God, which surpasses all understanding, will guard your hearts and minds through Christ Jesus"* (Philippians 4:6-7).

Desiring to perfect your faith, make this request known to the *Author and Finisher of your faith*. *"Looking unto Jesus, the author and finisher of our faith, who for the joy that was set before Him endured the cross, despising the shame, and has sat down at the right hand of the throne of God"* (Hebrews 12:2).

Are you in a bind and in the natural there is no way to meet this need? Humbly call upon the provision of *Jehovah Jireh, The Lord Who Provides:*

And He said, "Do not lay your hand on the lad, or do anything to him; for now I know that you fear God, since you have not withheld your son, your only son, from Me."

Then Abraham lifted his eyes and looked, and there behind him was a ram caught in a thicket by its horns. So Abraham went and took the ram, and offered it up for a burnt offering instead of his son. And Abraham called the name of the place, The-Lord-Will-Provide: as it is said to this day, "In the Mount of the Lord it shall be provided" (Genesis 22:12-14).

Is there a battle raging in your life that you need God to reveal Himself strong? Is this a battle that God has called you to fight? If so, claim the strategy and victory of our God with the name of *Jehovah Nissi, The Lord is my Banner* (Exodus 17:9-16).

Are you feeling worn down from your present battle? Is the devil bearing down hard upon you? Call upon *Jehovah Ma 'Ozi, the Lord our Strength* to overcome when and where you feel weak. *"The Lord is my strength and song, and He has become my salvation; He is my God, and I will praise Him; my father's God, and I will exalt Him"* (Exodus 15:2).

Do you now see the power in these different names of our God? These are just a few, there are many more to discover, but use the names here and add them into your daily fellowship with God. Learn to activate these specific powers and see a transformation in your prayer life as you begin to call upon these distinct character traits of Jehovah God.

Are You Missing Part of Your Armor?

Don't be like the warrior who is dressed for battle wearing the helmet of salvation, the breast plate of righteousness, the belt of truth, shoes of the Gospel of Peace, and is holding up the shield of faith, but is missing an important part of the armor—the sword.

God gives us this all-powerful, supernatural sword to defend ourselves in the daily skirmishes of life that rise up against us. But it cannot help us unless we first pick it up. In other words, we need to read the Bible, speak its written words aloud, and do what it says.

As we studied in chapter 1 from Joshua 1:8 *"This Book of the Law shall not depart from your mouth, but you shall meditate in it day and night, that you may observe to do according to all that is written in it. For then you will make your way prosperous, and then you will have good success."* Because according to Second Timothy 3:16-17, *"All Scripture is given by inspiration of God, and is profitable for doctrine, for reproof, for correction, for instruction in righteousness, that the man of God may be complete, thoroughly equipped for every good work."* And we are blessed when we obey it, *"Blessed are those who hear the word of God and keep it!"* (Luke 11:28).

Pick up your sword and overpower satan with the ultimate authority of God's Word. Worth repeating from the Epigraph in the front of the book, the Confession of Faith to Wield the Tongue is provided for you again.

Confession of Faith to Wield the Tongue

I wield the power of my tongue to heal and protect my faith in God so that it is not rendered useless (James 1:26), emulate Yeshua, the Living Word, and release prophetic healing by the power of my spoken words.

I bridle my tongue (James 1:26), to keep my soul from trouble (Proverbs 21:23). I will not speak of wickedness, or utter deceit (Job 27:4). I extinguish the fiery flames of hell (James 3:4-6), as I repent of a murderous tongue, and will no longer listen to or speak gossip (Romans 1:28-32; Proverbs 26:20), but will speak the truth in love (Ephesians 4:15).

I will not defile my body with negative speech and faithless words (Matthew 15:11), but will study God's promises to know how to give faith-filled answers (Proverbs 15:28), utilize the power of pleasant words that are sweet to the soul and healing to the bones (Proverbs 16:24), I will meditate upon the Scriptures day and night (Joshua 1:8), so that I will prosper in all things and be in health (3 John 1:2).

My speech is seasoned with salty grace (Colossians 4:6), His goodness that edifies (Ephesians 4:29), wholesomeness, like a tree of life (Proverbs 15:4), it brings forth wisdom (Proverbs 10:31), and spurs others to believe for their healing while it is still today (Hebrews 3:13).

Like Elohim, I create by words of faith (Genesis 1:1-4), I utilize the creative force of my tongue and give life to the dead and call into being that which does not exist (Romans 4:17).

With my voice I exalt the name that is above all names, Yeshua, Jesus, the King of kings, and the Lord of lords, and not the sickness or disease (Philippians 2:9-11). I openly give thanks because He is good, and His mercy endures forever (Psalm 118:1).

God Gives You the Responsibility to Bring about Change

Oftentimes, people cry out to God and ask Him to change the situation for them. But He has put this in our hands to do and has given us the "how to" instructions in His Manual. It's time to be responsible and open up the Book and bring about the change we need.

Let's pray: *"Dear Father God, forgive me. I am convicted by Your Spirit because I have not been in Your Word as I should have been. Holy Spirit, I ask that You would lead me and guide me as I start afresh in the Word today. In Jesus' name I ask, amen."*

As we study the Word, we find that there are numerous types of prayers listed in the Bible. We will review some of these in the next chapter. And I ask that you consider adding these types of prayers into your daily fellowship with God and start to activate victory in your life today.

Personal Word Checkup

Is my spiritual sword sharp or dull? If it's dull, am I willing to take the time to sharpen it? Am I spending quiet time in the Word every day? If not, what is hindering me from studying the Bible? Are there things I can eliminate to free up more time in my life to spend with God? When attacks come, am I ready to fight the battle and win? Or have I been living a defeated Christian lifestyle? Who is responsible to make the changes necessary in my life?

Group Discussion

What have we learned from this chapter about wielding our swords of the Spirit? Do we feel we need to sharpen our swords? What steps do we need to take to sharpen our spiritual blades? How can we open up more time to spend in God's Word?

Questions for Chapter 7— Wield Your Sword of the Spirit

1. According to Ephesians 6:12 what type of battle are we in on this earth?

2. If we cannot fight the things of the spirit in the strength of the flesh, then how do we fight these spirits?

3. How do we live in His victory against the wiles of the devil?

4. What do you need to rightly handle in order to wield your sword effectively?

5. What is a dull sword in the Kingdom of God?

6. What can't you do with a spiritually dull blade?

7. How do we first form a sharp edge on our spiritual sword, the prophetic and healing power of our words?

8. As we mature in the faith, how do we continue to sharpen our supernatural skills of the use of the Word?

9. How do we actually mature in the faith and sharpen our skills?

CHAPTER 8

PRAYER STRATEGIES

You have what it takes, you're born again, you live according to the Word of God, you've even been baptized in the Holy Spirit, but your prayer life suffers. Your prayers don't seem to be answered as they should—perhaps you are going at it the wrong way.

Just as words have distinct meanings and are used for different purposes, so too God has divergent types of prayer strategies recorded throughout the Bible, and they aren't there by chance, but for your purpose—to show you how to have success in your prayer life for particular situations. It's time to discover these precise types of prayer strategies and implement their power and create the change you so desire.

Word of the Lord

THE WORD OF THE LORD WOULD SAY TO YOU, *"Learn of the secrets of the Kingdom. Pray in the power of My wisdom and strength. You have suffered too long, but no longer need to. Be open to the teachings through My Word and know that when your words of faith line up with My Word, power is released and answers come forth."*

What Is the Purpose of Prayer?

Part of the plan of redemption is not only for your salvation, but to also restore the fellowship between you and God. In other words, He wants to commune, to have one-on-one fellowship with you. And this is the purpose of prayer—communication with God. Learn to experience genuine fellowship in your prayer life and pray the way God wants you to pray.

The Hebrew word for "pray" is *palal* (Strong's H6419) and means to intervene and interpose (intercede). Sometimes when you pray you share with Him about your needs and desires for yourself or for others, and we will investigate numerous different methods about how to do this effectively.

Individual or Corporate Prayer

You wonder, *How do I know when to pray by myself or when a matter should be prayed through in a group setting?*

Praying by yourself is the most common way to pray. It is one of the foundational ways you build relationship with God by communing with Him alone. There are times when people cannot pray with others, think of all the missionaries around the world, or your local pastors sometimes can't present their needs to those they minister to because the people are not always mature enough to understand the needs of a leader and their real need for privacy.

Other times, you may not be able to bring your prayer need to others because of the sensitivity of the issue and the damage that it may cause the one in need of prayerful intervention. Everyone does not need to know all that's going on in the private lives of others.

In these instances, God has not left them without anywhere to turn. They can turn to the Word of God and align their petitions in agreement to it and learn how to operate in the areas of decrees, binding and loosing, and praying in the Spirit. All of these prayer strategies will be discussed later on in this work.

Jesus talks about praying in secret or in private in Matthew 6:5-6:

And when you pray, you shall not be like the hypocrites. For they love to pray standing in the synagogues and on the corners of the streets, that they may be seen by men. Assuredly, I say to you, they have their reward. But you, when you pray, go into your room, and when you have shut your door, pray to your Father who is in the secret place; and your Father who sees in secret will reward you openly.

Corporate Prayer

But there are times when corporate prayer is the best and most effective option. In the Book of Acts we see how the early Church gathered together and prayed corporately: *"These all continued with one accord in prayer and supplication, with the women and Mary the mother of Jesus, and with His brothers"* (Acts 1:14). This is how the Church was born and grew in number.

It was also how they made decisions, choose Church leadership (Acts 6:1-6), and sent out their first missionaries (Acts 13:1-3). We also read in First Timothy 2:1-2 (NIV) where Paul is admonishing Timothy to incorporate this type of prayer in his gatherings:

I urge, then, first of all, that petitions, prayers, intercession and thanksgiving be made for all people—for kings and all those in authority, that we may live peaceful and quiet lives in all godliness and holiness.

A general rule of thumb: if it is a public matter, it should be prayed for corporately, if it is a private and sensitive matter, then it should be prayed for privately or in a group of two or three very trustworthy and mature individuals as a prayer of agreement. We will study this type of prayer strategy as we move further along in this chapter.

Prayer of Supplication

The Greek word for "supplication" is *deēsis* and means "a request or petition" (Strong's G1162); the biblical usage of this word is seeking, asking, and entreating from God or from man. And so a prayer of supplication is asking or petitioning God for something. It is also a personal prayer request for yourself.

Philippians 4:6-7 (AMP) gives us a clear explanation how to actuate a prayer of supplication:

> *Do not be anxious or worried about anything, but in everything [every circumstance and situation] by prayer and petition with thanksgiving, continue to make your [specific] requests known to God. And the peace of God [that peace which reassures the heart, that peace] which transcends all understanding, [that peace which] stands guard over your hearts and your minds in Christ Jesus [is yours].*

On the authority of Philippians 4:6-7, this is how you should make a request or petition for yourself. Remember to include the elements of faith we clearly see in these verses.

- Do not be worried or anxious about anything, this includes a negative report.

- Activate the prayer of faith.

- Make your specific petition known with the power of thanksgiving.

- Let the peace of God rule over your mind and emotions.

Example of the Prayer of Supplication

Dear Father God,

In the name of Your most holy Son, Jesus, I come boldly before Your throne of grace, and with the prayer of faith I make my petition with a heart of thanksgiving known to You. I do not beg and plead, but I thank You for Your faithfulness to perform Your Word on my behalf. I thank You for Your healing power that flows within my bones, and that my marrow is recreated and healed. It is strong again and produces healthy red blood cells, and my blood is cleansed from the sludge of this disease. My body is disease-free and will remain this way all the days of my life. And according to Your Word I stand on the promise that I will live to be a ripe old age full of strength and joy. I will fulfill my destiny and bring You much pleasure, and the share the relief of Your healing power to others.

In the mighty name of my Healer, Jesus, amen.

Prayer of Intercession

As we discovered, a prayer of supplication is to make a request or petition for ourselves, whereas a prayer of intercession is to pray on the behalf of others. And this truly is a labor of love; you could spend this time and pray for your own needs, but instead you lift up the needs of another. And it follows right along the lines of Jesus' selfless example for us in that He is at the right hand of God and intercedes for us (see Romans 8:34).

> *First of all, then, I urge that petitions (specific requests), prayers, intercessions (prayers for others) and thanksgivings be offered on behalf of all people, for kings and all who are in [positions of] high authority, so that we may live a peaceful and quiet life in all godliness and dignity* (1 Timothy 2:1-2 AMP).

In Genesis 18:23-32, we read the account of how Abraham intercedes for Sodom and he and God make an agreement that if there were at least ten righteous people, the city would be saved, but there were not even ten godly people to be found and the city of Sodom with Gomorrah were destroyed because of their wickedness. But this is an excellent example of how we are to intercede on the behalf of others.

Prayer of Intercession for Revival Dear Father God,

You promise in Second Chronicles 7:14 that "If My people who are called by My name will humble themselves, and pray and seek My face, and turn from their wicked ways, then I will hear from heaven, and will forgive their sin and heal their land."

We cry out for forgiveness for being stiffed-necked and rebellious toward You and Your ways. We admit that we have walked away from Your Word and from Your ways of holiness. Jesus, we have crucified You again and again by our willful acts of sin. As the Church in general, we have lowered the bar and have matched our standards with that of this world. We have made a mockery of the most sacred and central doctrines of the Church. Holy Spirit, we have grieved You, and we have lost our way, lead us back to the Way, the Truth and the Life.

We desire a spiritual bath, like no other time of cleansing we have ever experienced before. No matter how much it hurts, reveal the spots and wrinkles so we can remove every hint of stain and rid ourselves of even the slightest wrinkle. We desire to make ourselves ready for You, our soon and coming Bridegroom.

We have been selfish in the giving of our time, finances, and other resources. We pledge to do our part and take care of the orphans and the widows in their time of need. Forgive us; we will clean up our act and do the work of the ministry, and not burden our leaders with all this business so they can devote themselves to the study of the Word and prayer.

As Your people, we humble ourselves and pray for our brothers and sisters in Christ, both young and old, who live near and far, who are weak in the faith—that Your Spirit of conviction will hover over them and not let them go. Daily woo them to a place of repentance and in right standing with You. Bring the people who will capture their attention in such a way that they listen. May they make amends with You and others they have hurt. And may they grow in the faith, through the Word and by the Spirit, and become all that You destined them to become for Your glory and purposes.

We pray for the leaders of this land, whether we voted for them or not, that they may come to know You as Savior and follow after Your ways in both their personal and public lives. And may they make decisions based upon Your agenda and not that of their own.

Again, we ask for Your forgiveness and this time for entering into the hate speech of this world. We know better, and are reminded that faith only operates by love, and one way we show love to others is with our words. We have completely missed it in this and have stopped our own miracles and those of our family and friends as well. We vow to make a 180-degree turn and we will not be instruments of satan's hate, but that of Your love.

May the leaders in the church rise above the atmospheric pressures of this world and bow on bended knee before You. May they study to show themselves approved onto You, workers who do not need to feel shame. And may they preach the truth of Your Word with all boldness and lead the people to You and to Your righteousness.

We lift up the marriages within our churches, that these couples will choose to love and cherish one another, and walk daily in the arena of forgiveness.

May the children be won back to You and surpass our generation spiritually in the name of Jesus. May they hear and obey Your voice and witness Your mighty hand upon their lives.

Forgive Your people of our land of the murderous thoughts and intentions and actions they have committed, from the abortion of their own flesh and blood, to assisted suicides.

Forgive those for vile sexual acts. Help these lost individuals find their way back to the natural and godly use of their bodies as You originally designed and intended for us.

We see this world is winding down, and we have not been open to do our part, but there is a change within us, and we desire to be used for Your glory and to be about Your heavenly business and win people to the matchless wonder of Your name.

Hear us, oh God, forgive us of our sin and heal our land.

In Jesus' name we humbly pray, amen.

Prayer of Faith

Some would have us believe that God has left us stranded in the middle of nowhere, with little help offered by Him. But this is not the character or nature of our God. He's the opposite. He has bequeathed to us a spiritual medical chest full of supplies to help us in our very time of need. No matter the situation or how bad the medical report is, He's supplied us with a complete medical healing kit, including the basic first aid supplies for spirit, soul, and body—the names of Jesus and the power of His blood. And right next to these basic supplies is a packet called Faith, with an instruction booklet on how to open the special seal:

1. In order to open this specially sealed faith packet you must first believe.

2. Beliefs are voice activated—open your mouth and speak words of faith.

3. Then act upon the words you speak.

Now, let's open this medical healing kit and find out what it has to say about the prayer of faith.

What Is Faith and the Prayer of Faith?

First we have the matter of faith. What is it? Certainly it's not feelings. According to Hebrews 11:1, *"Now faith is the substance of things hoped for, the evidence of things not seen."* Faith is a supernatural foundation, it literally upholds you. Its strength depends upon your relationship and communication with Elohim, the Father, Son, and Holy Spirit.

Interestingly, James refers to something called the prayer of faith in his writings. We would think that when we pray we use faith, but apparently this is not always the case. Much of what is said during prayer is not faith at all. Let's face it, there is a lot of whining, complaining, and blaming going on during prayer.

And how many times have you heard it said in prayer, *"If it be Your will..."* There is no faith activated in a prayer like this. This statement shows that the heart is not settled upon God's will in the matter. It reveals insecurity and a lack of trust in the God who truly cares for your needs.

This is especially true when it comes to prayer for healing. If we do not know the will of God to heal, we cannot pray with faith and believe that God hears us and responds to us according to our words full of faith. This is why we spent time in the last chapter discussing how important it is to sharpen the blades of our spiritual swords.

Let's continue on with our study about the prayer of faith.

So Jesus answered and said to them in Mark 11:22-24:

> *Have faith in God. For assuredly, I say to you, whoever says to this mountain, 'Be removed and be cast into the sea,' and does not doubt in his heart, but believes that those things he says will be done, he will have whatever he says. Therefore I say to you, whatever things you ask when you pray, believe that you receive them, and you will have them."*

We see in these verses that in order for prayer to work, you must first believe, have faith for your healing, and trust in the faithfulness of God to move on your behalf. In Mark 5:34 (AMP) Jesus says to the woman, *"Daughter, your faith [your personal trust and confidence in Me] has restored you to health; go in peace and be [permanently] healed from your suffering."* Without faith, prayer doesn't work.

Then you speak to the mountain, the situation or the sickness attacking you. You command it to be removed from your midst, or from your body.

It may take time for the situation to change, but regardless of the time involved, you must remain strong in the faith and believe you receive what you pray for. If you will, this mountain will remove itself far from you.

And again we have confirmation about the successful results of the prayer of faith or when prayer and faith are combined. James confirms to us, *"The prayer of faith will save the sick, and the Lord will raise him up. And if he has committed sins, he will be forgiven"* (James 5:15). As mentioned previously, many people pray, but not necessarily with faith. But prayer mixed with faith is very powerful, and here it heals the sick. Read the following testimony about how the prayer of faith heals a woman's sick kidneys.

Kidney Disease Healed by the Prayer of Faith

I recently prayed with a woman who suffered from kidney disease. She was very sick and her body did not function properly. I released the prayer of faith into her kidneys and commanded them to be healed and to function normal, in the name of Jesus. With tear-filled eyes she shared with me the next day that her kidneys were functioning and she used the restroom all day. Glory to God. This is a wonderful testimony of what happens when two or more will agree together in the name of the Lord and release the healing power of the Holy Spirit with a prayer of faith.

You say, "Yes, Becky, but that's your calling. Of course you have results when you pray." Hmmm...I have several ways I can respond to such a comment. First, regardless of my calling I have to stir my faith like anyone else and believe that God's healing power works.

Second, part of my calling is not only to minister healing to the sick, but to empower you with the healing message and with the power of the Holy Spirit. Just like I have been discipling the woman in the next testimony, I am doing the same with you. Teaching you how to pray in faith and to believe that when you do—healing happens.

Stage 4 Lung Cancer Healed by the Prayer of Faith

A young lady I have been mentoring over the past couple of years received a message from a friend a couple of months back requesting prayer for his dad's best friend who had been diagnosed with stage 4 lung cancer with no treatment options. She began to pray and told her friend what to pray. (Just as I had taught her in my books and healing seminars.) Friday, he messaged her and said thank you for the prayers. There is NO cancer!

What did she tell her friend to say and do? She told her friend to renounce the spirit of death attacking his lungs and any negative medical diagnosis spoken over him. And she encouraged him not to doubt that he is healed, but to stand on the healing promises of God. And that he needed to be in agreement with these words of faith.

Just as the prayer of faith worked for this man, it will work for you too.

Healing Scriptures to Add to Prayers of Faith

- *The Lord will sustain and strengthen him on his sickbed; in his illness, You will restore him to health* (Psalm 41:3 AMP).

- *O Lord my God, I cried to You for help, and You have healed me* (Psalm 30:2 AMP).

- *Behold, I will bring it health and healing; I will heal them and reveal to them the abundance of peace and truth* (Jeremiah 33:6).

Basic Prayer of Faith for the Sick

In Jesus' name, we believe in the healing power of Jesus, our Healer for our (brother or sister) in the Lord. We command this disease to stop harming them, and that (name of the person) is delivered and healed from this sickness. No longer can this illness remain in the body. By the blood of Jesus, it has lost its stronghold on our dear loved one. We declare that (name of the person) will live and not die, but will rise up from this sickbed healed and will testify for the glory of our Lord. In Jesus' name we pray in faith and believe that all things are possible, amen.

I believe it is time to move forward in the healing power of the Holy Spirit and set free with a prayer of faith those who suffer from the ploys of the devil and usher them into the Kingdom of God.

Now, let's take a look at the prayer of worship.

The Prayer of Worship

I believe there is a bit of confusion between praise and worship among believers. According to Strong's concordance 3029, the word "praise" in the Hebrew language is *yeda,* and it means to give thanks. And whether we praise in song or in prayer, there is an element of jubilee with it. The word "worship" in Hebrew is *sebó* (Strong's 4576) and it means to personally esteem; to hold something (someone) in high respect; showing the reverence or awe (veneration) of someone who is devout. And the physical position of the body is not that of jubilant dance, but often in a humble position down on our knees or prostrate before Him.

A prayer of worship centers on the person of God, who He is, rather than what He does or has done for us. Jesus teaches the disciples how to pray to the Father in what we call the Lord's Prayer in Luke 11:2-4, *"Our Father in heaven, hallowed be Your name."*

Around the throne of God we see in the Book of Revelation 4:8-11 that the four living creatures fall on their faces and cry out day and night, *"Holy, holy, holy, Lord God Almighty, who was and is and is to come!"* And then the twenty-four elders fall down before Him, and as they cast their crowns before Him they cry out in worship, *"You are worthy, O Lord, to receive glory and honor and power; for You created all things, and by Your will they exist and were created."*

Oftentimes as I worship with my heavenly language, I will hear the interpretation in my natural language pour forth from my mouth. And I will hear these very words coming from the depths of my spirit, *"Holy, holy, holy is the Lord God Almighty, who was and is and is to come." And this is where worship comes from*—the depths of the heart, and it is very sacred in nature. It's intimate, up-close and personal.

I believe we should spend most of our prayer time in worship. And even when we say a quick prayer we should open up to the Father with words of worship.

Worship Scriptures

- *Oh come, let us worship and bow down; let us kneel before the Lord our Maker* (Psalm 95:6).

- *Give unto the Lord the glory due to His name; worship the Lord in the beauty of holiness* (Psalm 29:2).

- *But the hour is coming, and now is, when the true worshipers will worship the Father in spirit and truth; for the Father is seeking such to worship Him. God is Spirit, and those who worship Him must worship in spirit and truth* (John 4:23-24).

Prayer of Worship

Dearest Almighty God,

I cry out from the depths of my heart, "Holy is Your name. You are high above the heavens and greatly to be praised. There is no one who can match Your greatness. I worship You in spirit and in truth. You are the very breath that I breathe; You are the reason that I live. You are my Maker and my Master, and I stand in awe in the beauty of Your holiness.

You are not a plaque on the wall, a statue on a stand, a cross around my neck, or a charm in my pocket. You are the real, authentic, and living One, and nothing can compare with You. My eyes are fixed on You, and You alone. I hear the whisper of Your voice and I eagerly reply, "Here am I." I see the revelation of You in Your Word, and the more I seek You, the more I find You. Therefore, I meditate upon Your Word, and upon You day and night.

I travel the earth, and everywhere I go You are with Me. You are faithful and true; You never leave me nor forsake me. I witness Your compassion—Your love in action for all people in all places. And still my favorite place in all the world is to be alone with You.

If I find myself in the valley, I walk straight on through to the other side with You. If I stand at the foot of the mountain, I climb to the top with You. When it is time to come down from that mountain-top, I come down with You. You are always at my side. And You never leave me nor forsake me.

I was hungry for Your righteousness and am satisfied. I tasted of Your goodness and am blessed beyond measure. I was thirsty and You gave me water from the eternal well that never runs dry.

I love You with all that is within me, because You are love and You first loved me. In the midst of deep trials and misunderstandings, You are my peace that surpasses all understanding. You are my joy and my strength, and I love to laugh with You.

You are the new song, the melody that I sing. Every note with You is in perfect pitch and in harmony with Your Word. And whether I sing with choirs of angels or solo, what I sing, I sing about You.

I am confident in Your faithfulness. You are not a man who lies. You eagerly wait to perform Your Word. You are my steadfastness in an ever-changing world. And I take comfort that You are steady and true and You never change. I can always depend upon You.

Lord, You are my rock, my Protection, my Savior. You are my stronghold in the day of trouble, You are my Deliverer from all affliction, You are my shield and my saving strength. Great are You, my Defender.

I live to worship You, amen.

Now that we have viewed the prayer of worship, let's research the prayer of praise and thanksgiving and how to apply this to our daily prayer life.

Prayer of Praise and Thanksgiving

As I mentioned earlier, praise means to give thanks in Hebrew. And this is how we will approach the topic of praise and thanksgiving in prayer.

Colossians 4:2 admonishes us to *"Continue earnestly in prayer, being vigilant in it with thanksgiving."* I believe one reason Christians become burdened down with worries and strife is because they cease to be thankful and praise God for all that He provides. Sometimes you need to stop, if even for just a moment, and consider what the Lord has done for you. First Thessalonians 5:16-18 reminds us to *"Rejoice always, pray without ceasing, in everything give thanks; for this is the will of God in Christ Jesus for you."* Have you ever noticed that truly happy people are those who appreciate the simple things in life?

Another reason for discontentment is that God's people don't serve Him—they serve a spirit of mammon, and with mammon comes materialism. And materialism is empowered by a spirit of lust that desires more and more of something. And things, no matter how much pleasure they bring, are only temporal—paper tears, plastic melts, glass breaks, and iron rusts. Along with greed, materialism instills jealousy and unnecessary competition. Too often brothers and sisters in Christ, with greedy assumptions, think they should start out in a life of ministry at the same level of someone who has been faithful to ministry for 40-50 years. And usually these young ministers get themselves in a whole lot of financial trouble. Greed is often the reason that ministries and marriages fail. Materialism cannot buy true happiness.

Learn to cultivate a heart of thanksgiving, being content where you are, and with what you have.

Thanksgiving Scriptures

- *And whatever you do in word or deed, do all in the name of the Lord Jesus, giving thanks to God the Father through Him* (Colossians 3:17).

- *Enter into His gates with thanksgiving, and into His courts with praise. Be thankful to Him, and bless His name* (Psalm 100:4).

- *Oh, give thanks to the Lord, for He is good! For His mercy endures forever* (Psalm 107:1).

Let's take this moment and thank Him for nonmaterialistic things in life. And then make it a habit to thank Him every day for something that money cannot buy.

Father God,

I take a moment and look around at all that You provide me with and I thank You for it all. I am thankful for the air that I breathe. And every breath is a moment in time that I will not be able to go back and relive, so with a thankful heart I live this moment for You. I will not waste my time and complain about frivolous things that have no eternal value—I will cherish all that I do have.

I thank You for the beauty in Your creation that You give to me to use and enjoy. I thank You for the sun that shines, the ocean that roars, the flowers that bloom, the birds and the butterflies that fly, the stars that shine, the moon that gives light in the night sky.

I will not complain where You plant me. I am thankful for the seasons, the freshness of spring, the pleasantries of summer, the bountiful harvest of fall, and the glistening snows of winter.

I am thankful for: eyes that see Your artistic beauty in nature; ears that hear its music You orchestrate for me; fragrant aromas I can smell and enjoy like lilacs, raspberries, pine needles, fresh basil, and oregano. For the ability to taste the sweetness in a strawberry, the tartness of a fresh lime, and the saltiness of the ocean air, and for hands that touch the amazing textures of this life.

I choose to relish in this moment with my Creator, Elohim. You have blessed me beyond measure with things that are not manufactured by human hands, but with loving thoughts and creative commands.

Thank You for giving me this moment to voice my thanksgiving to You, in Jesus' name, amen.

Instead of complaining about material things that you do not have at the moment, write down a dozen things here that you are thankful for, and spend a thanksgiving moment and thank the Lord for these God-given creations.

1. _____

2. _____

3. _____

4. _____

5. _____

6. _____

7. _____

8. _____

9. _____

10. _____

11. _____

12. _____

A Prayer of Thanksgiving for Healing before the Manifestation

I would like to write an example of prayer of thanksgiving for healing with the added element of faith before the manifestation of the healing takes place. I think it is important to know how to pray with thanksgiving while we wait and stand in faith for our healing.

Dear Father,

I thank You for giving to me a measure of faith. And as I cultivate this faith in You and in Your healing power, all things become possible to me, including my healing. And as my trust in Your promise to heal grows, so too my faith to believe grows.

I align my thanksgiving for my healing with this promise found in Jeremiah 17:14, "Heal me, O Lord, and I shall be healed; save me, and I shall be saved, for You are my praise."

I thank You for giving me a free will to believe, for taking my shame upon Yourself, for wearing the crown of thorns so I am now delivered from the curse, for shedding Your blood for my healing at the whipping post, for wearing the crown of thorns so I can be delivered from the curse, for releasing Your blood through Your hands so I can now have this blessing of healing, for spending all that You had so I could have all of Your benefits. For completing the work of the cross for my well-being in spirit, soul, and in my physical body. I thank You, Jesus, for shedding Your blood for me at the whipping post so I can live on this earth in a healed state.

Your Word tells me that it is by my faith I am healed. So I activate in advance my faith in Your healing promise that tells me that by the whippings of Jesus I am healed, and so I am.

In Jesus' name, amen.

Prayer of Agreement

Jesus shares another prayer strategy in Matthew 18:19-20, He says, *"Again I say to you that if two of you agree on earth concerning anything that they ask, it will be done for them by My Father in heaven. For where two or three are gathered together in My name, I am there in the midst of them."*

The exciting element of this prayer is that Jesus arrives on the scene, but only after we do our part. And that's if two or three will gather together in His name and are in complete agreement about a matter for prayer. There cannot be any hidden agendas in this, you are to be in 100 percent agreement with one another—and this is to be done in His name, not in the name of a church, organization, or in the name of an individual, but in the name of the Lord.

The presence of Jesus will manifest in the midst of these few believers who are gathered together for a common purpose. I often teach people how to create a miracle, and one main ingredient necessary is the presence of God. Genesis 1:1 says, *"In the beginning God created the heavens and the earth."* In the beginning of any miracle you must have God at the starting line. He's the Alpha and the Omega, the beginning and the end. He's also the Author and Finisher of our faith.

And here Jesus, Himself is telling us how to have guaranteed success in prayer, gather two or three people together and come into agreement with every aspect of the request. And He will join you in this prayer request.

Jesus sits at the right hand of the Father and already makes intercession for the saints. Hebrews 7:25 says, *"Therefore He is also able to save to the uttermost those who come to God through Him, since He always lives to make intercession for them."* It reads this way in the Amplified Version of the Bible, *"Therefore He is able also to save forever (completely, perfectly, for eternity) those who come to God through Him, since He always lives to intercede and intervene on their behalf [with God]."*

What a beautiful and electrifying thought to consider that while you are praying the prayer of agreement just like He teaches you to do, that the presence of Jesus is right there with you, joining and praying with you.

This means your requests are being heard not only in Heaven, but by Jesus Himself, and then He presents the request to the Father. Now, that's good news!

We're now going into another prayer strategy called Binding and Loosing Prayers.

Binding and Loosing Prayers

"And I will give you the keys of the kingdom of heaven, and whatever you bind on earth will be bound in heaven, and whatever you loose on earth will be loosed in heaven" (Matthew 16:19).

There are numerous types of prayers recorded in God's Word and they all serve a specific purpose and accomplish certain goals. In binding and loosing prayers, there are very strategic points to note.

Jesus starts off by telling Peter and the others, *"I will give you the keys of the kingdom of heaven."* This is quite the gift to say the least, let's investigate this further to gain a clearer understanding of what is being said here.

According to Strong's G2807, "keys" in Greek is *kleis*. And it is the keeper of the keys who has the power to open and to shut; in the New Testament, this is a metaphor and denotes power and authority.

The Greek word for "kingdom" is basileia (Strong's G932), and it means royal power, kingship, dominion, and rule. This is not to be confused with an actual kingdom but rather the right or authority to rule over a kingdom. This speaks of the royal power of Jesus as the triumphant Messiah, conferred on Christians in the Messiah's Kingdom.

"Whatever you bind on earth will be bound in heaven, and whatever you loose on earth will be loosed in heaven." It is important to note that the initial action starts here on this earth with you. All too often God's people wait for Him to deal with the difficult situations we face in this life. But again we see here that God leaves the responsibility in your hands. You are the one responsible to bind the strongman rising against you.

The Greek word for "bind" is *deo* (Strong's G1210). And what does it mean to bind? It means to tie, fasten with chains, or to throw into chains, to forbid, or prohibit something. Satan binds people by the means of demons as he did to the woman who was bent over with a spirit of infirmity for eighteen years (see Luke 13:10-17).

So you can see when you bind the enemy you forbid and prohibit him and actually throw him in chains, thus exercising your authority in Christ, and then you need to use the spiritual tool of loosing.

The Greek word for *loosing* is *lyo* (Strong's G3089). And this means to loose any person or thing that is tied or fastened to someone or something; to set free or release someone who is bound up. For example, someone who is bound to a demon, you loose them from this spiritual stronghold in the name of Jesus. You deprive the enemy of his authority over the individual and overthrow or overtake them with this Kingdom principle.

Jesus demonstrates this power of binding and loosing when He heals the blind and mute man in Matthew 12:22-29 and explains this Kingdom principle to us when He rebukes the Pharisees for their unbelief in His ways. He explains in verse 29, *"How can one enter a strong man's house and blunder his goods, unless he first binds the strong man? And then he will plun-der his house."*

The strongman is satan and his demons, and they bind you to their wicked works such as sickness and disease. And before you can plunder his domain and take back what he has stolen from you—your health—you take this key of binding and loosing and activate your God-given authority and bind him up, tie him up, and take away the power that he has used against you.

To use this Kingdom principle, you must align your binding and loosing with God's Word. It is the only way it can operate. In other words, it has to be in 100 percent in agreement with Scripture.

This type of prayer is not a permanent fix. You can't bind the spirit of sickness from never trying to attack you again. You will have to learn to develop your faith vocabulary and use it daily to protect yourself.

Here is a sample of a binding and loosing prayer for the protection of your family:

> Jesus, as You say in Matthew 16:19, You gave to me the keys of the kingdom, and whatever I bind on earth is bound in heaven; therefore, I bind satan and his demonic force and their wicked efforts to try to steal, to kill, and to destroy my family. I declare Isaiah 54:17, "No weapon formed against us shall prosper." I loose the supernatural protection of the Father through the atoning blood of the Lamb. In Jesus' name, it shall be so, amen.

This has been a powerful time of study in the area of prayer strategies to strengthen our spiritual use of our words in prayer. Now, in the name of Jehovah Rapha, let's put His healing power into practice.

Verbal Elements of Faith to Heal

Let's activate the prophetic and healing power of our words and work these verbal elements when we speak or pray in faith: decrees, declarations, binding and loosing, prophesying, and create the healing and miracle we have need of in our physical bodies, in Jesus' name.

Feet, Knees, Hips

Feet

I decree in the name of my Physician, Yeshua: "He makes my feet like the feet of deer, and sets me on my high places" (Psalm 18:33). I bind the strongman of a crippling spirit and loose the healing of my feet. And I prophesy that my toes are straight and pain free. My nails are well fortified, they do not crack, peel, or splinter and they are free from fungus. My arches are not deformed, they are reformed and they withstand great pressure. My ankles do not give in, they support my stance. I decree that my feet are delivered from all abnormalities and arthritis, and they are beautifully reformed. And I align my words with God's promise in Romans 10:15, "How beautiful are the feet of those who preach the gospel of peace, who bring glad tidings of good things!" *and this includes my feet.*

Knees

In the name of Jesus, my Healer, I decree God's Word over my knees: "Therefore strengthen the hands which hang down, and the feeble knees, and make straight paths for your feet, so that what is lame may not be dislocated, but rather be healed" (Hebrews 12:12-13). I bind the strongman, a lame spirit, and I loose the power in the name of my Healer, Jehovah Rapha. I release creative power into my knees as I prophesy that they are healed and made whole. The newness of the Spirit flows into my bones, muscles, ligaments, tendons, and nerves. My kneecaps are refreshed, free from spurs and abnormalities. I have the full amount of cartilage necessary. They are free from disease and healed from injuries. I can bend and stretch freely. I line up my words with God's healing promise from Isaiah 40:31 and decree as I "wait on the Lord I shall renew my strength; I shall mount up with wings like eagles, I shall run and not be weary, I shall walk and not faint." I confess by faith my knees are healed for the glory of God, amen.

Hips

I decree that death and life are in the power of my tongue. I bind the crippling strongman attacking my hips and loose the power of Jesus' blood at the whipping post for my healing. And in Jesus' name, my Physician, I prophesy that these hips are free from the curse of disease and pain. My pelvic area and the pelvis bones are realigned, the ball and socket joints are recreated, pain free, and function perfectly normal. I can bend over and touch my toes, sit down and stand up freely, even stand and walk for great lengths of time with ease, and when I lie down to sleep they are at peace, and my sleep is sweet and pain-free, in Jesus' name.

Spine

I decree Jesus' words of freedom from Luke 13:12, "I am loosed from this infirmity." In Jesus' name, my Healer and Deliverer, I prophesy that I have a strong and healthy back, my spine does not shrink with age—it remains straight and full of strength. My spine is realigned, the disks and vertebrae are recreated and made whole, this spine decompresses every day. My spine is free from pain and disease.

Neck

In the name of Jesus, my Healer, I decree Matthew 18:17 over my neck, "He Himself took my infirmities and bore my sicknesses." I declare that Jesus is my Healer. I bind the strongman, the thief who comes to steal, to kill, and to destroy my neck, and I loose the abundance of the life of Jesus to flow into it. I prophesy health and strength into my neck and that any and all forms of muscle strains, worn joints, nerve compressions, injuries, and diseases are healed, and my neck is made whole for God's glory and for my good pleasure, amen.

Autoimmune Disease

I decree Isaiah 53:5 over my immune system, "by His stripes I am healed." I bind the strongman, the spirit of death, and I loose the Spirit of Life into my body. And in the name of Jesus, my Physician, I prophesy into my immune system and say you may not produce antibodies that attack my own tissues, but only those that fight off infections. My immune system no longer attacks and kills my body, it does what it is designed to do—heal itself for the glory of the Lord.

Multiple Sclerosis

In the name of Jehovah Rapha, the Lord who heals, I bind the strongmen, the spirit of death and MS, and they stop attacking my nerve cells. I loose the Spirit of Life to flow into my immune system. I decree that "by His stripes" my nerve cells are healed, and I am delivered from MS and premature death. I prophesy life into my entire body, no longer do I suffer pain, blindness, weakness, poor condition, or muscle spasms. My body can only align itself to the power of the suffering of Christ for my healing at the whipping post and that by His shed blood I am healed, in Jesus' name, amen.

Rheumatoid Arthritis

I decree Genesis 1:26 over my body in Jesus' name, "I am created in the image of God." I bind this strongman, Rheumatoid Arthritis, and loose the healing power of the Holy Spirit and my immune system is healed "by His stripes" and does not harm me. I prophesy that my immune system is made whole and am at peace with myself. It does not produce antibodies that attach to the linings of my joints. My joints are not inflamed, swollen, or in pain, they are healed and made whole; and in the name of my great Physician, Jesus Christ, I declare Luke 13:12 that "I am loosed from this infirmity," amen.

Allergies

In the name of Jehovah Rapha, my God who heals, I decree that my faith in the atoning blood of Yeshua has healed me as it says in Luke 17:19. I bind this strongman of allergies and loose the power of the Holy Spirit to heal. I prophesy that my sinuses are realigned and healed, they are not supersensitive, not inflamed, infected, or afflicted in anyway; they are free from infection, irritation, pain, and function perfectly normal, in the name of Jesus, amen.

Eating Disorders

Anorexia

With the keys of the Kingdom of Heaven, I bind a spirit of death and lying spirits against my image. I renounce harmful and destructive behaviors against myself. I loose the power of the Holy Spirit to heal me in spirit, soul, and in my physical body too. I declare that I am free from past abuse and the damage of hurtful words and actions. I am no longer controlled by self-hatred or suicidal thoughts. I forgive those who have hurt me, I release them from my bitterness and from my vengeance. And in doing so, I am forgiven and healed from the inside to the outside, in Jesus' name. The mirror does not determine my image—Jesus does. And as He is so am I, beautiful in every way. With this newfound revelation in Jesus, I am no longer anorexic, but delivered and healed in His name.

Malnourishment, Digestive Problems, or Wasting Away from Disease or Medication and Treatments

I bind the strongman of death in my life; I loose the Spirit of Life in me. I prophesy that my appetite is healed and I am hungry now. I will not waste away and die. I will live life to the fullest. I can eat, hold down food, and gain weight. I will no longer degrade my appearance; I declare that I can maintain a healthy weight for my height and bone structure, in Jesus' name.

I bind the strongmen of death and disease in my body. I loose the healing power of the Holy Spirit to flow within me. I prophesy that my digestive system is realigned, healed, pain-free, and recreated from all damage caused from disease, medications, and medical treatments, and it functions per-fectly normal, in Jesus' name.

Bulimia

In Jesus' name, I bind the strongman of death and destruction against me. I loose the healing power of Jehovah Rapha, my Healer to flow in me. I prophesy that I am free from past abuse, the damage of hurtful words and actions. I am no longer controlled by self-hatred or suicidal thoughts. I forgive those who have hurt me, I release them from my bitterness and from my vengeance. And in doing so, I am forgiven and healed from the inside to the outside, in Jesus' name. When I look in the mirror, I see Jesus, as He is so am I, beautiful in every way. With this newfound revelation in Jesus, no longer do I overeat. I do not binge and purge my food. Food is no longer my source of comfort—Jesus is.

Digestive Diseases

Inflammatory Bowel Disease (IBD)

I decree Matthew 8:17 over the lining of my intestines, "He Himself took my infirmities and bore my sicknesses." I bind the strongman of IBD and command it to stop attacking the lining of my intestines. I loose the healing power of the Holy Spirit to flow in them instead. I prophesy in the name of Jesus, my Healer that I no longer suffer from episodes of diarrhea, rectal bleeding, urgent bowel movements, abdominal pain, fevers, or weight loss. Nor do I or will I suffer from Ulcerative colitis or Crohn's disease, because "by His stripes I am healed and made whole."

Irritable Bowel Syndrome (IBS)

In Jesus' name, I decree Luke 13:12, that I have been loosed from this infirmity, IBS. And that "by His stripes" my large intestine is healed from cramping, abdominal pain, bloating, gas, and diarrhea and constipation. I prophesy to my body and I say that the muscle contractions in my intestines are normal, the nerves in my digestive system are at peace, there no longer is a problem with inflammation, and I have the proper amount of immune-system cells in my intestines. In the name of Jehovah Rapha, I do not suffer from infections from bad bacteria or viruses. I do not have a surplus of bacteria in my intestines; rather, I do have the exact amount of microflora, the good type of bacteria I need for healthy intestines; in the name of the Lord, I am healed, amen.

Acid Reflux

In the name of Jehovah Rapha, my Healer, I bind the strongman of sickness and disease and acid reflux. I loose the power of Jehovah Rapha that heals me. I prophesy that my lower esophageal sphincter (LES) is recreated and healed. And it opens and closes properly in the name of the Lord. I activate the authority of Christ over this situation and no longer do I suffer from heartburn, because I am healed totally and completely by the blood of Jesus, amen.

Crohn's Disease

In the name of Jesus, I bind the strongman of death, disease, and Crohn's disease from stealing my health, killing my body, and destroying my life. I loose the abundant life of Jesus to flow through my digestive tract. I prophesy in the name of the Lord that I am free from abdominal pain, inflammation, severe diarrhea, fatigue, weight loss, and malnutrition. I decree the healing promise of the stripes of the Lord in Isaiah 53:4-5 deep into the layers of my bowel tissue. And by my faith in the healing power of the Lord, I am healed and made whole, amen.

Heart and Lung Diseases

Cardiovascular Disease

In the name of Jehovah Rapha, I call on the creative power of my Lord, Jesus Christ. With the keys of the Kingdom of Heaven, I bind up the strongman of cardiovascular disease from destroying my heart and the workings of it. With these same keys I loose the dunamus power of the Holy Spirit to flow throughout my entire heart to recreate the four chambers, the artia and the ventricles. And the right atrium and the ventricle work to pump oxygen-poor blood to the lungs, and the left atrium and ventricle combine to pump oxygenated blood to the body,[1] in Jesus' name. And the septum is strong and divides the right and the left ventricles and does not allow the mixing of oxygenated and deoxygenated blood.[2]

In the name of my Creator, Jesus, the four different layers of my heart—the pericardium, the epicardium, the myocardium, and the endocardium—function properly, each one functioning as it should, and aids the pumping action of the heart to allow my blood to flow properly.[3]

I receive this same dunamus power to recreate the four valves within my heart—the tricuspid, the pulmonary, the mitral and the aortic valve—and they do the jobs each was created to do, to open when the blood passes through them and then close to keep the blood from flowing in the wrong direction.

The conduction system of my heart functions perfectly normal as Elohim created this system to operate; my heart rate is set perfectly and allows the upper and lower chambers to communicate with each other so they can function in a coordinated fashion, for the glory of the Creator of my heart.[4]

I decree God has not given to me a spirit of fear. I will not fear having an attack of the heart or stroke, because in Jesus' name my blood vessels are not narrowed or blocked, they are open and free as they should be. I declare Isaiah 53:4-5, by His stripes my heart is delivered and cleaned from cardiovascular disease, healed, strengthened, and functions perfectly well in the name of the Lord, amen.

Asthma

In the name of Jesus, I activate my faith. I bind the strongman, asthma, from working against the proper function of my lungs. I release the dunamus power of the Holy Spirit to clear out my lungs from this disease. I prophesy over them that they are strong and healthy. I breathe easily, my airways are not narrow or swollen. My lungs do not produce excessive amounts of mucus, only what is normal and healthy. I decree Second Timothy 1:7 over myself; I do not possess a spirit of fear, but of power and of love and of a sound mind. I do not fear premature death by an asthma attack, because according to Hebrews 2:15, Jesus released me from a lifetime bondage to the fear of death. And by His stripes this asthma was whipped out of my body as He took it upon His for me. And because my faith is strong in the name of my beautiful Healer, Jehovah Rapha, I am delivered and healed from asthma, amen.

Chronic Obstructive Pulmonary Disease (COPD)

In the name of my Healer, Jesus Christ, I activate my faith in the keys of the Kingdom of Heaven, and I bind and evict this strongman of COPD that has inhabited my lungs. With this same key I loose the dunamus power of the Holy Spirit and give Him all the space in my lungs to inhabit, to flow in and out from. I decree that at the whipping post this sickness was whipped out of my lungs as Jesus took COPD into His lungs for me so I could be free from this disease by the shedding of His blood for me.

No matter the cause, whether by my willful sin of smoking, or by other means, my lungs are free from COPD. And all other labels, if emphysema, my air sacs (alveoli) where weakness or rupture has occurred, they are recreated. And instead of larger air spaces, the curse has been broken and they now many small air spaces as God intends them to be. My alveoli work properly and old air is no longer trapped, but I now have room for fresh, oxygen-rich air to enter.

If the label is chronic bronchitis, my bronchial tubes are healed, no longer inflamed and can freely carry air to my lungs,[5] in Jesus' name. If the label is Agent Orange, by the blood of Jesus my body is cleansed from this deadly chemical and no longer has the power to work in my lungs or any other part of my body. My lungs and my entire body are free, healed, and strengthened by the mighty power of the blood of Jesus. And from this moment forward, every breath I take is a testimony of the magnificent healing virtue of the Great Physician, Jehovah Rapha, Himself. I declare that by His stripes I am healed from COPD.

Other Diseases

Diabetes

In the name of Jesus, my Healer, I bind the spirit of death and diabetes from having its way in my pancreas. I release the creative, dunamus healing power of the Holy Spirit and by the healing stripes of Jesus, my pancreas is recreated and healed in the name of Yeshua. I will not settle for the devil's lies or lying symptoms of type 1 or type 2 diabetes. No, by faith I am healed and made whole. My pancreas is recreated and functions perfectly normal. In the name of my Healer, Jehovah Rapha, amen.

Cancer

Jehovah Rapha, You are the Lord who heals me as you say in Matthew 16:19, you gave to me the keys of the Kingdom, and whatever I bind on earth is bound in Heaven; therefore,

I bind satan and his demonic force and their wicked efforts to try to steal, kill, and destroy me with this wicked cancer. I bind cancer and the spirit of death from destroying my health and strength, and from killing off my physical body. I bind the spirit of fear from stealing my peace, my hope, and my faith. I stand firmly planted on the Word of God that declares "by His stripes I am healed"; therefore, according to Your instructions I loose my promised healing by the redemptive blood of Yeshua, my Healer. In Jesus' name, I decree I am healed, amen.

Human Immunodeficiency Virus (HIV) and Acquired Immunodeficiency Syndrome (AIDS)

In the mighty name of Jesus Christ, I bind the spirit of death and the HIV virus attacking my immune system. I command you, HIV, to leave my white blood cells, my T-helper cells in my immune system alone. You do not have my permission to reproduce yourself within my CD4 cells. The original HIV cell and its copies are not allowed in my body. Death, you will not have your way with me. I decree the word of the Lord over myself from Psalm 118:17, "I shall not die, but live, and declare the works of the Lord." I loose the Spirit of Life and the dunamus healing power of the Holy Spirit to flow freely throughout my entire body.

I prophesy into my body that "by His stripes," my blood is washed clean, and by my faith I am made whole. The HIV count within my body goes down to zero, not one count as the world believes, but down to zero, as the blood of Jesus decrees, and never rises within my body again.

My immune system is recreated with brand-new white blood cells, my CD4 cells are stronger and healthier than they have ever been. In the name of the Lord, I fight off all infections, bad bacteria and viruses, and opportunistic diseases quickly and easily.

By my faith I declare that my immune system is recreated, healed, strong, and is able to fight off any and all infection and disease. I am alive and well, in Jesus' name, amen.

This has been a good study in God's Word about different prayer strategies, and we have learned a lot to help us to become more effective in the use of our spiritual words in the area of prophetic and healing power. Now, let's go to the next chapter and learn strategies for deliverance from various evil spirits.

Personal Word Checkup

Do I have what it takes to access success in my prayer life? Am I born again? Do I live according to the Word of God? Am I baptized in the Holy Spirit? Do I pray in tongues? Do I pray in tongues on a consistent basis? Does my prayer life suffer? Do I feel my prayers are being answered as they should be? Have I been activating any of these faith elements and prayer strategies in my personal prayer life? Or are most of these things new to me? Am I willing to activate these faith elements and prayer strategies? Do I value the different names of Jesus? Do I activate the powers of His different names in prayer? Am I willing to start afresh and do so now? Do these spiritual tools excite or overwhelm me? If I find them overwhelming, am I willing to take it slowly and add one new faith element at a time?

Group Discussion

How do we feel about these faith elements and prayer strategies? Will we start to implement them in our prayer lives? Have we been using the different names of Jesus when we pray? Do we know of other names of Jesus we can add to our prayer lives? What one prayer strategy are we going to start to use straight away? Why? How do we believe it will make a difference?

Questions for Chapter 8—Prayer Strategies

1. In the plan of redemption, what else besides salvation does God want to restore? What is the Hebrew word for "pray"? What does it mean?

2. What's the general rule of thumb to help you decide if a matter should be prayed for privately or corporately?

3. What is the Greek word for "supplication"? What does it mean? What is the biblical usage of this word?

4. Is the prayer of supplication used as a personal prayer request or a prayer request for others?

5. Who do we pray for with a prayer of intercession?

6. According to Hebrews 11:1, what is faith?

7. What does faith's strength depend upon?

8. What is the prayer of faith?

9. What is the Hebrew word for "praise"? What does it mean? Whether we praise in song or in prayer, there is an element of what with praise?

10. What is the Hebrew word for "worship"? What does it mean? Oftentimes, what is the physical position of the body when we worship?

11. Who does the prayer of worship center on?

12. What does Matthew 18:19-20 tell us about the prayer of agreement?

13. In Matthew 16:19, what does Jesus give to us?

14. What power does the keeper of the keys possess?

15. What is the Greek word for "kingdom"? What does it mean?

16. What power are you given with a prayer of binding and loosing?

17. What is the Greek word for "bind"? What does it mean?

18. What is the Greek word for "loosing"? What does it mean?

Note

Hebrew and Greek word definitions are provided by Strong's Concordance and can be found at Blue Letter Bible: https://www.blueletterbible.org.

Endnotes

1. Cincinnati Children's, "Heart Components" https://www.cincinnatichildrens.org/health/h/components; accessed April 24, 2018.

2. Life Easy Biology, "What is the Function of the Septum in the Heart?"; http://www.biology.lifeeasy.org/3916/what-is-the-function-of-the-septum-in-the-heart; accessed April 24, 2018.

3. Ken Hub, "Layers of the Heart"; https://www.kenhub.com/en/library/anatomy/layers-of-the-heart; accessed April 24, 2018.

4. Cincinnati Children's, "Heart Components"; https://www.cincinnatichildrens.org/health/h/components; accessed April 24, 2018.

5. Mayo Clinic, "Emphysema"; https://www.mayoclinic.org/diseases-conditions/emphysema/symptoms-causes/syc-20355555; accessed April 24, 2018.

CHAPTER 9

DELIVERANCE STRATEGIES FROM VARIOUS SPIRITS

Because the power of our words are so very strong that they not only possess life and death, they also open us up to sickness and disease, and all sorts of problems, even demon oppression and possession. We are going to consider strategies for deliverance from various types of demonic spirits.

As I am preparing my heart to start to write about deliverance from various spirits, I look up from where I am and in the sky I see a warring angel with his sword in hand and he is fighting off a devilish beast. My kids are near me, and I tell them to look at the sky and tell me what they see. They all can see the very same thing. In amazement we watch what happens in the spirit realm. And truly *our struggle is not against flesh and blood [contending only with physical opponents], but against the rulers, against the powers, against the world forces of this [present] darkness, against the spiritual forces of wickedness in the heavenly (supernatural) places"* (Ephesians 6:12 AMP). Interesting to me, the weapon of choice is the sword of the Spirit. And this very same weapon is placed in our hand to battle these demons every day of our lives.

We have to accept the fact that certain battles are more difficult because some demons are stronger than others, but we still use the same weapon, the spoken Word of God; but the strategies will be different and much more intense according to the direction of the Spirit.

You may feel a sense of fear and intimidation about standing up to demons and casting them out of someone, but God expects His people to do the work of the ministry. The following are a few verses to personalize your authority in Christ to do this.

- *I can do all things through Christ who strengthens me* (Philippians 4:13).

- *As Jesus is so am I on this earth* (1 John 4:17).

- *I have been given the authority to trample on serpents and scorpions, and over all the power of the enemy, and nothing shall by any means hurt you* (Luke 10:19).

Now, take this God-given authority in Christ and exercise your clout and dominate the demons and the situations that manifest themselves against you and those you love.

A Jezebel Spirit

A Jezebel spirit is a very complicated spirit to tangle with, but you must rid it from your midst. Revelation 2:20-22 warns us what will happen if we do not rid this wicked spirit from our fellowship:

> *Nevertheless I have a few things against you, because you allow that woman Jezebel, who calls herself a prophetess, to teach and seduce My servants to commit sexual immorality and eat things sacrificed to idols. And I gave her time to repent of her sexual immorality, and she did not repent. Indeed I will cast her into a sickbed, and those who commit adultery with her into great tribulation, unless they repent of their deeds.*

You will always find a sexual link somewhere in the life of the individual who is suffering from possession of a Jezebel spirit—it goes with the spiritual territory of this demon.

Accept the fact in advance that if you choose to do what's right and take a stand against this demon, you will be lied about, your personal calling, gifting, and authority will be challenged and questioned, you will be dishonored, and along with the Jezebel demon, a vengeful spirit will rise against you. But we can take comfort now in Romans 8:31 (AMP) and know that *"If God is for us, who can be [successful] against us?"* This is a very sly and deceptive spirit, and you probably will not recognize it at first, until you question a comment or response or an action made by the person. In the situation I had to confront, the trouble started when I disagreed with a prideful remark made about herself while she tore down all the other team members. And all I said was, "I'm sorry, but I can't enter into this type of conversation with you. As a leader, it's wrong for me to speak against our team members. And you may have had more training than some of the others, but they have more experience than you do. I will not speak against them."

In a normal situation, this conversation could have been resolved with a little bit of repentance, "Oh, I see your point. And yes, you're right we should not speak against one another. Forgive me. I will work on this." But you see, it was not a mere disagreement. This was more than dealing with someone who was acting too big for her britches. I did not realize at that time that I was actually dealing with a person consumed with a demon called Jezebel. And its plan of action is to befriend the authority of a ministry, especially one that ministers in the prophetic. The secret mission of this demon is to steal what they have, to kill off the one in the office of the prophet, and to destroy their work of the Lord. This demon is very dangerous and highly deceptive.

Even before I disagreed with the woman this day, she had handed me a teaching from a series of teachings about prophets. It was not the complete series, just one session about the shortcomings of a prophet. I thought her gesture was strange and rude at the same time. The situation left a negative taste in my mouth.

Soon after I had dared to disagree and speak up in peace, everything I said or didn't say was being twisted and used against me. Even this person's time in the Bible was being twisted against me. And as I mentioned earlier, this demon is as sly as a fox and just as destructive as one in a henhouse. It will go after what God has birthed through you. It will do everything in its power to ravage your nest.

At one point, this person even offered to buy out the ministry. I ask you, "Can you purchase the workings of the Holy Spirit from another?" No, you can't. We read in Acts 8:18-24 about a great sorcerer named Simon who was now born again, but immature in the faith and was covetous of the power Peter and John walked in. He made them an offer he thought they couldn't refuse, but to his surprise he was rebuked for his carnal and sinful ways. He found out—and we need to know this basic principle as well—the gifts and the callings of the Holy Spirit are not for sale.

This spirit is not a low-level demon. It ranks high in satan's kingdom. And it has destroyed many ministries, many marriages, and many families. And everywhere it goes—it steals, kills, and destroys.

The only way to combat this secretive demon is in the realm of the supernatural. I have never prayed so hard for any one individual in the ministry as I had for this particular person. Whether you want to admit it or not, if you are in the ministry, you have enemies—the devil will make sure of that. And they come dressed in disguise, hidden from the natural view. They are spiritual predators, wolves in sheep's clothing. This demon will act out as if it is the victim, when in actuality it is the perpetrator. And it is sent to devour the leaders, to take the ministry down.

The effects of this spirit works like a sticky spider web and it captures many victims. Anyone who could possibly threaten its security to be in control of other people, and if someone does not sell out their integrity with Jezebel's bribes and abuse the person, will be despised. Even if they have never been given a position of authority over others in the ministry, the position to control is the prized possession.

This woman with the Jezebel spirit was even caught pretending that our ministry was her ministry.

This particular person suffering from a Jezebel demon tried to influence other workers, volunteers, board members, and others in administration. Successful with some, others would not bow to these demonic ploys.

Someone with this demon will lie, cheat, and steal. This one stooped so low as to lie to the children she had been overseeing and told them lies about their birthmothers so they would never want to try to reconcile with them if ever given the chance. People bound to a Jezebel demon will bribe and manipulate with gifts, and often with large gifts or large sums of money to worm their way into the lives of unsuspecting people, to the point that people feel obligated to remain silent about the bad things they see going on.

They will pretend you are their new best friend—until you disagree with them and then you instantly become their worst enemy, and they your worst nightmare.

They go after the people in the ministry with the prophetic calls and gifts in operation. Why? Because the prophetic is the spirit of prophecy, the testimony of Jesus, see Revelation 19:10. And the prophetic and healing power of words, Jesus' words, possess the *dunamus,* dynamite explosive power of the Holy Spirit. It produces dramatic and oftentimes instant transformations—miracles in the lives of people. The enemy is terrified when God's people tap into the realm of the Holy Spirit, so he tries to silence the testimony of Jesus in you. Don't allow him to destroy you, your loved ones, your spouse, your family, your pastor and other leaders, or your ministry. Take spiritual action.

During this demon attack, I prayed in my native tongue and in my heavenly language daily. I interceded for this person's repentance. I prayed she would have a revelatory moment and would recognize the hand of the enemy in her life, and that she would cry out to God for help, seek God's forgiveness and inner healing, and would transform into a true and loving disciple—not a phony and covetous one—by the power of His redeeming love.

This is how we should pray in the beginning for the individual, as *"the Lord is gracious and full of compassion, slow to anger and great in mercy"*

(Psalm 145:8). God gives His people time to respond to the Holy Spirit's bidding to repentance. And this is the focal point of your intercession in the beginning.

If the person with the Jezebel spirit will admit having a serious problem without making excuses or placing the blame on another, then you move forward into the realm of repentance and restoration. The person needs to be removed from any place of ministry until it's proven the person can be trusted again, but with a strong element of accountability the second time around.

Unfortunately, it doesn't always turn out this way, people are not so willing to admit they have a problem with a demon spirit. But there comes a point, if they are not willing to harken to the voice of the Holy Spirit, that suddenly and swiftly supernatural action takes place, and strategies change.

As I shared earlier, I prayed in every way I knew how to pray. I searched my heart, I fasted, and had others join me that I could trust in this quest to find freedom and peace from the wickedness of this evil plot against me, my marriage, my family, and ministry.

One evening while praying in the Spirit, the Lord spoke to me and advised me how to take this spirit down. He said, *"You are praying the wrong way. Now, instead of commanding this Jezebel to hold its tongue and to behave itself, you need to pray this way: 'In Jesus' name, I command you to rear your ugly head and come against the others in administration so that they can see and hear clearly and know without a shadow of a doubt what I have been warning them about.'"* I immediately used the power of faith-filled words and *decreed* exactly as He had just instructed me. And the next morning it happened, its rebellious ways heeded my release to rebel against the others in administration. And this person was gone within a week.

There are times we need to change our prayer strategy, and the Holy Spirit will give this new strategy to us in His timing. The Lord is very patient, but He knows when His wooing process to the call of repentance is over. It has to do with the hardening of the individual's heart, when the person absolutely refuses to repent before God. And only the Spirit of God knows when this time comes.

And during this time, I personally met with two pastoral couples and asked them to pray and minister over me the way the Lord would have them to do. And they did, and they too saw into the prophetic realm and saw all that I had been suffering from. I remember toward the end of this ministry time, one of them saw my spirit being filled with daggers from the enemy. And as they prayed they pulled them out one by one. It was emotionally and physically painful. And then they saw a giant size dagger in the middle of my heart, and they commanded it to release me; when they were done praying, I felt an angel come and pull that huge dagger from my heart. It hurt so much physically as he did that I cringed and let out a sigh of pain.

I share this personal story with you because I often receive prayer requests from people who are suffering the attacks from someone possessed with a demon of Jezebel. So, it's time for more of us in the ministry to speak up and let others know that what they are dealing with is real, they are not imagining the attack. Even the pastoral couples who ministered to me suffered in the past from this very type of attack. And this attack is not of God. It's a demon working through another person to destroy you and what God has called you to do for Him, but there is help—Jesus, your Deliverer.

This demon does not just work through women, it also works through men. And in men it is very sexual and the men behave like predators, because they have given themselves over to a male Jezebel spirit. They are addicted to pornography, they have one affair after another. They are very charismatic in nature, people like them, until they get to know them better. Because they then start to see that there is a sexual problem in their life. A male Jezebel demon is after the man's marriage, to destroy the wife and children and ultimately the man who is possessed with this demon. It also operates in the life of unmarried men as well.

The following are steps to overcome this powerful demon—whether the one possessed is a man or a woman:

1. Pray in your earthly language and in your supernatural language (tongues).

2. Fast to break the stronghold this demon has against all those involved.

3. Pray earnestly that the person suffering with this demon possession repents and finds his or her way either to God or back to God.

4. Involve other mature Christians that can agree with you in prayer and fasting according to God's Word.

5. Forgive and release the person from your vengeance.

6. Pray daily earnestly.

7. Keep a listening ear for changes in prayer strategy. The Holy Spirit will lead you and guide you through all of this.

8. Pray that this demon of Jezebel is seen by others for what it truly is—evil and wicked.

9. Seek personal ministry with mature believers you can trust to pray you through inner healing.

10. Accept the fact that the person suffering from this demon of Jezebel may or may not repent. God gives them this choice. You work on yourself and keep your heart pure before God in this matter.

If you are not familiar with Jezebel or need a refresher course, read her story that is recorded in Kings chapters 1 and 2 in the Old Testament. And remember, no matter how bad the situation looks, God is faithful and true to His servants. He will deliver you from this wicked attack. Trust and believe that His Word with prayer and fasting work.

A Prayer of Protection to Pray over Yourself

In Jesus' name, no weapon formed against me shall prosper. I renounce you foul wicked spirit of Jezebel. You are not welcomed nor allowed to remain in my marriage, my family, in my ministry, or in my business.

I plead the blood of the Lamb, Jesus, over my mind and my emotions. I keep thoughts stayed on the Word of God. I meditate upon the Scriptures day and night. I live out the Scriptures and I shall not be moved from my place of peace with God.

I pray a hedge of protection around others who do not understand who or what they are dealing with. And those who have fallen into cahoots with this one, I ask, Father, that You will forgive them for they do not know what they are doing. Holy Spirit, hoover over everyone involved, may their spiritual eyes and ears of understanding open so that they may see and hear the wooing of Your Spirit to get out of the situation before it's too late for them.

I command you, Jezebel, to rear your ugly head at the others involved and you will expose yourself to the others. They will see you for what you really are—a demon.

Holy Spirit, cleanse the camp, no matter how large or small it may be, cleanse us spiritually of this filthy spirit.

In Jesus' name, I intercede, amen.

A Spirit of Lust

During the healing line, a man in his 70s makes his way to the front for several reasons, but before physical healing, he wants to repent from a spirit of lust. I lead him in a prayer similar to this one:

Dear Father,

Forgive me for sexually lusting after women. I repent of this wickedness. I know it's evil and not pleasing to You. I will to be free in Your precious name. I confess this sin and I believe in the power of Your forgiveness, not only to forgive me of this sin, but to deliver me too.

In Jesus' name, I am forgiven and set free, amen.

Now, when temptation comes, you need to choose to remain free from this sinful spirit of lust. Cry out loud,

> No, I will not lust after women. I have asked for the Lord's forgiveness and deliverance. And just as Jesus was tempted and did not sin, I will not sin at this temptation anymore. Holy Spirit, You say that You will not allow us to be tempted more than we can bear, so I am trusting and relying upon Your strength to stay clean from sexual sin.
>
> In Jesus' name, I declare freedom from a spirit of lust, amen.

A young teenage boy is surfing the Internet and up pops pornographic photos. At first he exits out of the site, but the spirit of lust starts to play games in his mind and he returns to the filthy site again and again. And one depraved thought leads to another and the young man is caught up in an addiction he never intended. Many of these young boys are raised in Christian families and have professed Jesus as their Lord, and some are even baptized in the Holy Spirit and pray in tongues. Many of these young men are up in the pulpits praising God openly in the service, but secretly living a life of sin at home.

These young men need deliverance. Sometimes all it takes is a prayer of repentance and accountability. Others are so bound by this strongman of porn they need the ministry of deliverance to be free from its demonic power. Whichever the case, they need spiritual help, because it is a spiritual problem—a demon. But greater is Jesus who is in us, than he, satan, who is in this world.

This problem has been around for a long time and it has been treated as a hush-hush topic. But it is time now for this message to be confronted from the pulpits, from the parents in the home, in Bible studies, and in Christian classrooms. As Christians, we need to put away the religious spirit that prevents us from exposing the truth in this matter and help our youth get free from satan's grip in this area.

Some claim this is a private sin and does not affect others, this is a lie from the enemy to give you an ungodly excuse to continue on in this sin.

It affects everyone, the society, the Church, the marriage, the family unit, the men, women, and children used in these pornographic forms of media.

If you really could see what you were lusting after you would run in the opposite direction—it's a demon in disguise, bent upon your destruction.

Women are coming forth in healing lines confessing their addiction to porn as well. And just like the men, the spirit of lust has them bound, it has no boundaries. It's no longer just with the opposite sex, but same sex addictions, and even sexual desires for little children.

God's people need a true revival to move through our midst. And revival starts in the heart of the individual. It begins with a prayer of repentance.

Let's pray: *"Father God, I come before You and confess my sins of sexual lust. I bind the strongman of pornography in my life, I release the Spirit of liberty and declare freedom from this sexual sin. Holy Spirit, I ask You to show me the demon behind this sick addiction. I desire freedom and whatever it takes to get free. I am willing to do things Your way. Expose this addiction to those around me so that my sin will find me out, so that I can confess my sins to them and find the spiritual help I need. In Jesus' name, I intercede for my deliverance, amen."*

Strategic Steps to Confront and Overcome the Demon of Lust

1. Prayer and fasting is a must for deliverance.

2. Remember, faith operates in love, not out of frustration, anger, or hate.

3. Honestly confront the one with the demon of lust.

4. Pray to God to forgive them for their betrayal.

5. Be patient and longsuffering and forgiving often.

6. Seek outside help from a mature and understanding Christian counselor.

7. Set up a strict system of accountability. Set up boundaries and consequences that you are willing to adhere to if need be.

8. Get rid of social media. You can actually live without it. Instead of a smart phone, invest in a flip phone. Lock up your computers, change your passwords, and invest in a secure Internet system that gives parents control over what is watched on the Internet.

A Spirit of Rebellion

The spirit of rebellion is another demon that is running rampant in both the world and in the Church in these last days. The enemy senses that his time is short to carry out his dirty business and so the demonic forces have increased in the strength of their fight against us. But glory to God we have the greater One living inside us who not only loves and cares for us, but leads and guides us through these battles victoriously.

Having said all of this, it still does not make it any easier for us to confront a spirit of rebellion in a wayward son or daughter, nephew or niece, a brother or sister, an out-of-control spouse, the next-door neighbor, a coworker, the pastor or missionary's kid, the students in the classroom, the volunteer who comes to so call, help at our mission, or Church. Wherever we are today, there is a spirit of rebellion everywhere we turn.

As with any other demonic possession or oppression, sometimes all it takes is true repentance, but other times the issues run much deeper than you realize and need ministry for deliverance and help from a professional.

A Strategy to Deal with a Rebellions Spirit

1. Pray and fast for wisdom for the reason for the rebellion.
2. Confront the issue in a spirit of truth and love, but not with passivity.
3. Remember your goal is to lead the person into repentance.
4. Be willing to repent if you have offended the person in any way.
5. Forgive the person for their wrongdoing.
6. Pray for the secret key to unlock their spirit toward you.

7. Give them a fair chance to make things right.

8. Seek out a Christian counselor if needed.

A Prayer for the Person Dealing with Rebellion

> In the mighty name of Jesus, I bind this strongman, a spirit of rebellion and its evil works to steal, to kill, and to destroy (name of person), and I loose the Spirit of Liberty to have its way. Holy Spirit, hover over them, convict them to repentance, and, Father, forgive them for they do not understand what they do and the evil that works within them. May their eyes and ears of understanding be open to Your truth. I decree Ephesians 6:10-11 that (name of person) is *"strong in the Lord and in the power of His might."* And (he / she) *"puts on the whole armor of God, that they may be able to stand against the wiles of the devil."* Romans 8:1 says that (name of person) *"does not walk according to the flesh, but according to the Spirit."* Romans 8:14-15 says, *"For as many as are led by the Spirit of God, these are sons of God. For (name of person) did not receive the spirit of bondage again to fear, but (name of person) received the Spirit of adoption by whom (he / she) cries out, 'Abba, Father.'"*

An Orphaned Spirit

People with an orphaned spirit come from all walks of life. They are not necessarily orphaned physically, but I know from having a children's home that these children do struggle with great hurts and wounded spirits. But as mentioned earlier, orphan spirits are produced from all levels of life. And emotionally they have painful wounds that have not been dealt with or healed. They feel rejected and fearful of people, they struggle with issues of abandonment and unworthiness. It's difficult for them to trust others and to receive and give true, godly love.

Orphaned-spirit people have a great need to be the center of attention. I believe this is the issue of school age children who are often labeled in school as being "the class clown," they lack the love and acceptance of an earthly father, so they act out seeking any attention given to them, whether positive or negative. And as they grow older, this need for attention grows deeper, and their means of seeking the center of attention becomes more sinful in nature.

In the children's home, the newer children come with predictable issues and behaviors; because they are in such need of physical attention, they either smother people until they are turned away by their behavior, or they shut down and force you to enter into their domain.

The fear of not being accepted is a major root issue to a sinful lifestyle. These people tend to be enslaved to sexual addictions, anything that gives them a temporal substitute for love, even if they are in the situation where they are now offered true, godly love. They are afraid that it is not genuine and run from it.

People with an orphan spirit rebel against authority. They want to be in control, even though they personally are so out of control. One sad trick that true orphans play is to deliberately behave so badly that others quickly reject them. It's a control game to get another to reject them on their terms before the person has a possible chance of doing it later on down the road.

They don't know how to be a son or a daughter, but they have a strong desire to be a father or mother, especially to the fatherless. But unless they are delivered and healed from this spirit, they will produce more orphan spirits, because they do not know how to parent in a healthy manner.

The orphaned spirit is fear based, and it is all about feeling unloved, unwanted, worthless, rejected, and abandoned. And until they come into the presence of their heavenly Father's love, and by His Spirit confront these past hurts, they will fulfill their spoken fears of failures to be loved, wanted, worthy, accepted, and adopted by others.

Three Scriptures about Spiritual Adoption by God

For as many as are led by the Spirit of God, these are sons of God. For you did not receive the spirit of bondage again to fear, but you received the Spirit of adoption by whom we cry out, "Abba, Father." The Spirit Himself bears witness with our spirit that we are children of God, and if children, then heirs—heirs of God and joint heirs with Christ, if indeed we suffer with Him, that we may also be glorified together (Romans 8:14-17).

For you are all sons of God through faith in Christ Jesus (Galatians 3:26).

Having predestined us to adoption as sons by Jesus Christ to Himself, according to the good pleasure of His will (Ephesians 1:5).

Ministry Strategy to Someone Bound by an Orphan Spirit

1. Pray and fast for them.

2. Love them and accept them as they are, faults and all.

3. Assure them that you adopt them into your life as a friend, son or daughter, as a valuable human being.

4. Earn their trust and love.

5. Set reasonable but firm boundaries of behavior for them.

6. Do not allow them to get away with rebellion.

7. Be a source of encouragement to be free from this demon spirit and to move forward without it in their lives.

8. Give them a reason to hope for something better with God.

9. Disciple them in the truth of who they are in God's Word.

10. Assure them they do not need to be perfect, no one is.

11. Lead them to Jesus, knowing that this might take time.

12. When they are willing, *minister the baptism of the Holy Spirit so they can build up their own spirits in prayer with the Spirit.*

A Prayer for Someone Enslaved to an Orphan Spirit

In Jesus' name, I lift up (name of person) to You, Father. I bind the strongman, the orphaned spirit that is afflicting (him/her) with lies of rejection and abandonment, fears of being unloved, unwanted and uncared for. I release the Father's love over (name of person) and the ability to trust and receive the Spirit of Adoption. I pray for them to have the strength and maturity to confront the past in a healthy manner. That this person would take on the mind of Christ and begin to filter past, present, and future events through the truth of Your Word. Surround (name of person) with godly people who will lead and guide (him/her) in godly love and acceptance. I intercede for the deliverance from ungodly behavior and addictions. I declare that You will become this person's Source of love, joy, and peace. That (he/she) will turn to You in times of loneliness and need and not to temporal fixes of this earth that profit nothing, only cause worse problems. In Jesus' name, I intercede for (name of person), amen.

A Vengeful Spirit

Let's face it, in this world bad things happen to good people. And when it does, there is great confusion, anger, and pain. But how do we rightfully deal with this situation? As painful as the situation may be, we need to do what's right according to the Word and forgive. Forgiveness is not based on hurt feelings, but on the atonement of Christ. And in order to heal, you must forgive. If not, you tie yourself to the evil that was done to you.

Let's look at rape. Perhaps you experienced this abuse; you didn't do anything to deserve it, no one ever deserves to be raped. You didn't ask for it, but it happened, and now you are a victim bound with pain, fear, anxiety, and hate. Something inside you wants the person to pay for what was done to you. And your mind thinks of painful ways to make the person suffer as you have suffered. But does this help? Does it bring forth your healing? Is this even biblical?

The answer is no. Revenge never heals the soul. It does not bring about physical or emotional healing either. There is only one way to be free from the evil done to you—forgiveness.

You say, "I can't do that." God says you must and you can with His help. You quickly respond, "Help? Where was He when I needed help?" The Word declares that *He will never leave us nor forsake us* (see Hebrews 13:5). You ask, "Why?" God gives to all people a human will, and with this will comes a great responsibility—choice. And when people are not right in their heart with the Lord and refuse to follow after His ways, they become self-centered and self-gratifying evil creatures, capable of doing serious harm to others. And this is what happens in the case of rape and other very grievous sins, they align themselves with the wickedness of the devil—the thief—and he uses these people to steal, kill, and destroy others (John 10:10).

But in the name of Jesus, you can learn how to forgive and be free from the bondage of their sin against you. You are not able to do this in your own strength, but with the power of the Holy Spirit you can be free from the sin of unforgiveness, revenge, and all forms of murderous thoughts and intentions. As long as you remain in the sin of unforgiveness, you will be unhappy, unfulfilled, fearful, and stunted in your emotional growth. Demons will visit you to haunt you in your thoughts and dreams, morning, noon, and night.

But Jesus, the bondage breaker, took upon Himself your pain so you can be truly free. Freedom from all this suffering is yours for the taking, but it starts with a quality decision to learn to forgive and to release the guilty party from your vengeance. God will show you how. He will lead you every step of the way. Don't allow the devil to steal from you any longer. Be free from this emotional prison and fulfill your destiny and become all that you were created to become.

Pray the following prayer by faith, not because you feel like doing so or that you think this person or persons deserve to be forgiven, but because God tells you that you must forgive them in order for your own sins to be forgiven.

Father God,

Forgive me for holding on to hate and unforgiveness, for harboring vengeful and even murderous thoughts. This is not who I am, or who I want to be. I desire to be free from this constant emotional pain. I admit this is not easy, but neither is the torment of unforgiveness and bad memories an easy road to walk down either. I have allowed my own bitterness, hate, and revenge to destroy my life even further. So by faith, I leave this negative baggage at Your feet. I don't want to carry this dead soul, my mind and emotions, upon my shoulders any longer. I give myself over to You. And this is the scariest step I have had to take thus far, but I willfully put my trust in You. Jesus, I know You are real, and I have placed the blame for much of this, if not all of this upon You.

Forgive me, I misunderstood that You are here to help me, and not to harm me. I lay this deep hurt at the hem of Your garment and I humbly say, "Take this from me. Show me how to be free, how to move forward with joy and victory. Help me to become all that You created me to become." And Father God, I have not known how to come before You with confidence. But right now, I am making a new start with You. Help me to become one with You, through Your Son, Jesus Christ. Holy Spirit, show me how to walk through this process of forgiveness and for once and for all be truly free from this day forward. In Jesus' name I take this first step of faith to find peace and freedom in You, amen.

I believe if you have prayed this prayer from your heart, then you have taken the first step; and as wobbly as it may seem, with each step forward you will become stronger and freer every day. The second step is to find a support group of believers in Jesus to walk this process with you.

Three Scriptures about Vengeance

Repay no one evil for evil. Have regard for good things in the sight of all men. If it is possible, as much as depends on you, live peaceably with all men. Beloved, do not avenge yourselves, but rather give place to wrath; for it is written, "Vengeance is Mine, I will repay," says the Lord (Romans 12:17-19).

Be angry, and do not sin: do not let the sun go down on your wrath (Ephesians 4:26).

So then, my beloved brethren, let every man be swift to hear, slow to speak, slow to wrath; for the wrath of man does not produce the righteousness of God (James 1:19-20).

A Strategy to Overcome a Vengeful Spirit

1.   Enter into a lifestyle of prayer and fasting.

2.   Read the Word of God daily.

3.   Live out the words of the Bible.

4.   Take a step of faith and forgive by faith.

5.   Ask the Lord to forgive you for having a vengeful heart.

6.   With the help of the Lord, release the person from your vengeance who has done evil against you.

7.   Join a Christian support group.

8.   Seek professional Christian counseling.

A Prayer for Someone Struggling with a Spirit of Vengeance

Father God,

In the name of Jesus, I lift up (name of person) to you. I bind the strongman in this person's life, a spirit of vengeance. I loose the revelation power of forgiveness over (his/her) life. Holy Spirit, hover over and woo this person into the realm of personal repentance of unforgiveness. Show how damaging this is to (name of person), and how it holds (him/her) in bondage to the person who has caused the harm when forgiveness is not given.

Show (name of person) how much you love and care for (him/her). And that You are their hope and answer—not the problem. Spirit and Truth, lead and guide this person every step of the way. I prophesy that (name of person) is free from the entanglement of a root of bitterness. And in Jesus' name we cut (him/her) loose from this root of bitterness.

Holy Spirit, lead (name of person) into the promised land of healing for Your glory, in Jesus' name, amen.

There are many demons that enslave people, but these are the ones that I believe the Lord would have me minister to you about in this work.

We've sharpened our spiritual swords again with strategies for deliverance from various demonic spirits. Now, we will continue to fortify the prophetic and healing power of our words as we learn to speak the same thing that God speaks in the next chapter, Confessions of Faith for Healing.

Personal Word Checkup

Can I identify with any of the demonic strongholds described in this chapter? Do I see myself as the victim or the perpetrator? Have I taken the steps necessary to be free from the stronghold that binds me to the one who has done me harm, such as forgiveness? Have I sought help from a professional Christian counselor? Am I involved in a Christian support group or Bible study group? Am I willing to use these prayer strategies to help me get free from this demon possession or oppression?

Group Discussion

As a group leader, discuss these sensitive issues with the group and be ready to minister to the needs of the people accordingly. You will need to be sensitive and led of the Holy Spirit in all of this.

Questions for Chapter 9—Deliverance Strategies from Various Spirits

1. What else besides life and death, sickness and disease, and all sorts of problems do the power of our words open us up to?

2. Even though some battles are more difficult and certain demons are stronger than others, what weapon will we use to combat these evil things? What will be different with the use of this weapon?

CHAPTER 10

CONFESSIONS OF FAITH FOR HEALING

A confession is a formal expression of your beliefs. In the Greek language, the word "confession" is *homologeó,* and it means to speak the same thing, or to agree (Strong's 3670). It is vital to choose to say the same thing God says with your confession. Instead of continuing to curse your body with negative medical reports, confess God's healing truths over your body. If you will be consistent with your confession of faith for healing, you will eventually see the manifestation of your healing come to pass.

Is it a lie to confess that *by His stripes I am healed* when you have symptoms? No, it is not. When you confess, you express your belief in something, and in this case you express your faith in the healing power of Jesus. The fact is that this sickness is an attack of the devil. It's a spiritual symptom with some form of illness attached to it. Remember, in reality, this is an actual spiritual battle, and things that exist in the physical realm, including physical sickness, disease, pains, and symptoms are temporal, but Kingdom principles are eternal, and you overpower this enemy when you use your spiritual weapons properly.

Instead of confessing the negative fact about satan's attack, confess the powerful truths of God's healing promises over yourself and allow the healing power to take root within you so that the manifestation can come into fruition.

Line up your words with God's vocabulary of victory and say what He says—and the power of your faith-filled confession will override satan and his wicked works employed against you.

Use the following list of Scripture faith statements and confess them out loud several times a day, just as if you were taking a dose of medicine for yourself or for someone else. Personalize these Scriptures, use your name, or the name of a loved one, and confess God's healing power.

- By His stripes I am healed (Isaiah 53:5).

- The Lord is my Healer (Exodus 15:26).

- My God has taken this sickness away from my midst (Exodus 23:25).

- The Lord has taken all sickness from me (Deuteronomy 7:15).

- Bless the Lord who heals all diseases (Psalm 103:3).

- I attend to His Word because it is life and health to my flesh (Proverbs 4:20,22).

- I am not afraid or dismayed, because the Lord my God is with me and strengthens and helps me (Isaiah 41:10).

- The Lord says He restores health to me and heals my wounds (Jeremiah 30:17).

- Jesus cast out the spirit with the Word and healed all who were sick. He Himself took this infirmity and bore this sickness (Matthew 8:16-17).

- Jesus went around healing every sickness and every disease among the people (Matthew 9:35).

- Jesus healed the lame, blind, maimed, and many others, and He has healed me, for which I glorify God, as the multitudes did (Matthew 15:30-31).

- Godly signs follow me because I believe. I lay hands on myself and others and we recover (Mark 16:17-18).

- Jesus gave me, as His disciple, power over all devils, to cure diseases, and to heal the sick (Luke 9:1-2).

- Jesus told us to heal the sick, so in obedience to Him, and in His name, I believe that I am healed, and know that the Kingdom of God has come near me (Luke 10:9).

- The Lord grants me boldness to speak His Word. He is stretches forth His hand to heal me in the name of Jesus (Acts 4:29-30).

- Jesus healed all of the sick people and those troubled with unclean spirits who were brought to Him. So, I bring myself to Him, and I am healed (Acts 5:16).

- God anointed Jesus with the Holy Spirit and with power. He went about doing good and healed all those oppressed by the devil, including me (Acts 10:38).

- God will keep me in perfect peace because my mind is fixed on Him and I trust in Him (Isaiah 26:3).

- I shall not die, but live, and declare the work of the Lord (Psalm 118:17).

Confessions for Young Children

We receive children of all ages in our children's home in Guatemala and I am always taken aback by how foul their mouths are when they come, and how quickly they infect the others with their negativity. In their formative years (the first five years of life), they have learned to insult, bully, cuss, and sass adults. The early years of life are so important, and as Christians we should do everything within our power to advance our children in the power of their speech.

For the sake of the children, start them out young in the prophetic and healing power of their words. Teach them positive confessions, that reinforce who they are in Christ, that keep them healthy, make them feel safe, and understand who they are in Christ instead of negative nursery rhymes and devilish stories that curse them and steal their peace of mind. Examples follow:

- Head and shoulders, knees and toes throughout my body His healing flows.

- I am strong and healthy in Jesus' name.

- With Jesus I am happy, healthy, and strong.

- Jesus keeps me safe all the days of my life.

- I sleep wrapped in peace and my dreams are sweet, in Jesus' name.

- I am not shy, I am bold like a lion. *ROAR!*

- I'm God's lamb, I'm not baaaah–d, but good.

- Jesus in me makes me free as a bee. *Zzzzzzz…*

- In Jesus' name, I am strong as an ox. Quick as a fox. My heart's soft like a bunny. And my words are sweet like a bee's honey.

- I fear not for God is with me.

- One, two, three—Jesus is with me.

- God made me a girl, and a loving mother may I be.

- God made me a boy, and with the love of a healthy father will I grow to be.

- I'm in God's army, a warrior of faith and prayer I am meant to be.

- Down on my knees, with my hands lifted up, I praise Jesus.

- My Jesus smiles at me.

- I am friends with my God.

- At any time, morning, noon, or night, I call on the name of Jesus and the devil takes flight.

- I believe—Jesus loves me.

Personal Word Checkup

Do I confess God's Word over myself? Or am I negative in my faith confessions in general? Do I confess evil over others as well as myself? Am I willing to change the way my words confess over others? What do I see as the most problematic area that I need to change my confessions over myself and others?

Group Discussion

Discuss the importance of lining up our confessions with God's Word. Choose a couple of confessions from the lists in this chapter to confess aloud every day until these confessions become a habit and they automatically come to your mind and out of your mouth the moment you open your eyes in the morning. Be ready to discuss the positive results a week, two or three weeks down the road together about how the confession of your faith-filled words have been changing your life, the life of your family, and the present situation you are in.

Questions for Chapter 10— Confessions of Faith for Healing

1. What is the Greek word for "confession"? And what does it mean? It is vital to choose to say the same thing God says with your confession. Instead of continuing to curse your body with negative medical reports, confess God's healing truths over your body. If you will be consistent with your confession of faith for healing, you will eventually see the manifestation of your healing come to pass.

2. What will happen if you consistently confess faith for healing over your body?

CHAPTER 11

DECLARATION OF FAITH

When you spiritually declare a thing, you make an official verbal statement about something you already have or possess. You declare your redemption in Jesus, the power of His blood, or other spiritual benefits such as: I have the mind of Christ. I do not have a spirit of fear, but of power, of love, and of a sound mind.

I travel in and out of Guatemala often for ministry purposes, and each time I have to fill out and sign an official document of what I have in my possession. I have to tell what I have, and sometimes I have to allow them to scan my luggage to prove what I say is true. This is a natural example of legally and truthfully declaring what I possess, and it works the same way in the spiritual realm; but instead of filling out a form, I verbally declare what I have, and I sign it with the name of Jesus. Oftentimes, what I declare will be tested to see if what I say is true. And it is the same for you too.

Not only does a declaration declare what you already have, it also encourages your faith and reminds you of your spiritual blessings.

As a mother, I can be at peace because I have a promise from God in Proverbs 22:6 that declares, *"Train up a child in the way he should go, and when he is old he will not depart from it."* No matter what my children pass through in life, I have in my spiritual possession the surety that my kids will not depart from the faith, because I have seeded the Word into them since they were infants and up until they went off to be on their own. Does this mean that they won't wonder off for a season? No, it means they will not depart from the faith. They will come back to their spiritual roots.

Let's look at another declaration we can claim as parents. God's Word declares in James 5:16, *"Confess your trespasses to one another, and pray for one another, that you may be healed. The effective, fervent prayer of a righteous man avails much."* My family knows that their mom often prays at night on our flat rooftop under the stars. They do not feel they are being cheated out of more Mom time, they actually feel my prayers are a safety net for the family.

Unknown to me at the time, one of our adopted sons, Andres, was being harassed that day by a demon spirit that appeared to him in the form of a human boy. It would appear and disappear. I could tell something was bothering him, and I even asked him if something was up, but for whatever reason he was not ready to speak about it yet—until that evening when I was up on the roof praying in the Spirit. He came running up the steps to the roof and said, "Good, you're here!" I could tell he was afraid of something and asked him to explain to me what was wrong.

He told me that while he was washing the vehicles that morning, a demon appeared to him in the form of a little boy. He would appear and then disappear in and around the vehicles. I was a little taken aback by the incident, but we prayed for an explanation for all of it. The answer came the next morning, another child in the children's home had brought home a local newspaper and in it was an article about the satanic game "Charlie," with instructions to teach children how to play the game. This other child had started to assemble the game, but for whatever reason never completed the act.

The newspaper was sitting on our dining room table without our knowledge about the content and the demon behind this wicked game tried to attach itself to the next unsuspecting child, which could have been any one of them, but it just so happened to be our miracle child, Andres.

Together, my husband and I and our children renounced this demon, and it did not appear to our son again, except we had to fight in the spirit realm against a spirit of fear that wanted to move in with our son, but we stood our ground and it left.

But that night I was up on the rooftop fervently praying for our son, actually standing above where he slept, and low and behold this demon appears on the boarder of our property seeking access to enter into the children's home. I saw him and I declared my covenant rights as a believer and the protection of the blood of Jesus and declared that *"No weapon formed against us shall prosper in the name of Jesus"*—and that demon left for good. I declare often that my fervent prayers avail much and they do for the glory of the Lord.

These are just a few examples of what happens when we declare what we already have in Jesus and how these declarations of faith produce results in the natural realm.

I Am Confident in My Identity in Christ

Too many of God's people lack the confidence they need in this life because they do not understand who they are in Christ and what He has given to them. Declare what you already have in Jesus with the following declarations of faith about your identity in Christ.

> I am created in the mirror image of the Father, Son, and Holy Spirit, Genesis 1:26, a little lower than Elohim, Psalm 8:5. I am set apart, Hebrews 10:10, from the rest of creation by the breath of God and have an eternal spirit, Genesis 2:7. I am an imitator of God, Ephesians 5:1, as Jesus is so am I on this earth, First John 4:17. Like Him, I have His authority to trample on serpents and scorpions, and over all the power of the enemy, and nothing shall by any means hurt me, Luke 10:19. I have dominion over every living creature on this earth, I am commanded to be physically and spiritually fruitful and multiply; to fill the earth and subdue it, Genesis 1:26-28.

I am a child of God, John 1:12, His special treasure, Exodus 19:5, fearfully and wonderfully made, Psalm 139:14, His workmanship, Ephesians 2:10, predestined and adopted into the sonship by Jesus Christ, Ephesians 1:5, accepted, Romans 15:7, lavished with the Father's great love, First John 3:1, inseparable from the love of God, Romans 8:38-39. I am part of the body of Christ, First Corinthians 12:27, complete in Him, who is the head of all principality and power, Colossians 2:10. He who is in me is greater than he who is in the world, First John 4:4. I am born of God, and the wicked one cannot touch me, First John 5:18.

He chose me before the foundation of the world, that I should be holy and without blame before Him in love, Ephesians 1:4. I am a friend of God, John 15:15, and an enemy to the devil, First Peter 5:8. I am inscribed on the palms of God's hands, Isaiah 49:16. I am loved, John 15:9.

My old self is crucified with Him, Romans 6:6. I am dead to sin, alive with Him, Ephesians 2:5. I am free from the law of sin and death, Romans 8:2. I am forgiven in His name, First John 2:12. I am redeemed, Revelation 5:9. My life has now been hidden with Christ, Colossians 3:3. I am born again, not of corruptible seed but incorruptible, through the word of God which lives and abides forever, First Peter 1:23, and I see the Kingdom of God, John 3:3. I am saved through faith, Ephesians 2:8. I am free indeed, John 8:36.

I am united and one in Spirit with Him, First Corinthians 6:17, brought to the fullness, Colossians 2:10. I am a living stone, First Peter 2:5, a chosen generation, a royal priesthood, a holy nation, special and called out of darkness into His marvelous light, First Peter 2:9. I am baptized and clothed with Christ, Galatians 3:27-28, a new creation; old things have passed away; behold, all things have become new, Second

Corinthians 5:17. I put on the new self, which was created according to God, in true righteousness and holiness, Ephesians 4:24 NASB. I am a disciple of Christ, I deny myself, take up my cross, and follow Him, Matthew 16:24.

I am a sojourner and a pilgrim on this earth, First Peter 2:11, a citizen of Heaven, Philippians 3:20. I am in this world, but not part of it, John 17:14-15.

I am a co-heir with Christ, Galatians 4:7, appointed to bear fruit, John 15:16. I am His ambassador, Second Corinthians 5:20, a minister of reconciliation, Second Corinthians 5:18, His fellow worker; field and building, First Corinthians 3:9. I am a temple of the Holy Spirit, bought and paid for with a price, First Corinthians 6:19-20.

I am Abraham's seed, an heir of the promise, Galatians 3:29. I am sealed with the Holy Spirit of promise, Ephesians 1:13, blessed with every spiritual blessing in the heavenly *places* in Christ, Ephesians 1:3.

I am a believer and have everlasting life, John 3:16. I cast out demons; I speak with new tongues; I will take up serpents; and if I drink anything deadly, it will by no means hurt me; I will lay hands on the sick, and they will recover, Mark 16:17-18.

I have the mind of Christ, First Corinthians 2:16.

I am bold as a lion, Proverbs 28:1. I am trusting toward God, Second Corinthians 3:4. I am strong and courageous, I am not afraid, or dismayed, for the Lord my God is with me wherever I go, Joshua 1:9. I am never alone, Matthew 28:20.

And I am the righteousness of God, Second Corinthians 5:21, holy and blameless before Him, Ephesians 1:4, justified by faith, Romans 5:1, redeemed from the curse, Galatians 3:13. And I am more than a conqueror, Romans 8:37.

I am the light of the world, a city set upon a hill, Matthew 5:14. Rooted and built up in Him, established in the faith, Colossians 2:7. Called to a holy calling, Second Timothy 1:9. I am the salt of the earth, Matthew 5:13, and all that I do, I do for His glory, First Corinthians 10:31. In Jesus' name, it shall be so, amen.

Write a list of twelve things you possess spiritually.

1. _____
2. _____
3. _____
4. _____
5. _____
6. _____
7. _____
8. _____
9. _____
10. _____
11. _____
12. _____

We've seen how we declare things that we already have in Christ, now in the next chapter we will learn to decree things according to the Word of God and see how they produce what they are spoken forth to do.

Personal Word Checkup

Do I make the regular habit of declaring what I have in Christ? Do I encourage myself with reminders of what I already possess spiritually? Am I willing to start this today?

Group Discussion

Discuss what you possess spiritually. Remind each other of the importance of remembering what you already possess in Christ.

Questions for Chapter 11—Declaration of Faith

1. What do you do when you spiritually declare a thing?

2. What else does a declaration do besides declaring what you already have?

CHAPTER 12

DECREES OF FAITH

What Is a Decree?

The word "decree" in Hebrew is *gazar,* and it means to cut, to divide, or to separate (Strong's H1504). And this is what happens in the spirit realm when we decree something. Job 22:28 (KJV) says, *"Thou shalt also decree a thing, and it shall be established unto thee: and the light shall shine upon thy ways."*

In Genesis 1:4, God decrees a separation between the light and the darkness: *"And God saw the light, that it was good; and God divided the light from the darkness."* In this instance, Strong's H914 matches the Hebrew word *badal,* and it means to separate, distinguish, differ, divide as in asunder, make a separation.

We see the usage of this concept throughout creation as far as dividing the waters from the waters, the firmament from the waters, and day from night. Or in Exodus 26:33, where God gives instructions to hang a veil to divide or to separate the holy place from the Most Holy. In Leviticus 10:10, this word is used to distinguish the difference between holy and unholy, clean and unclean. Isaiah 59:2 talks about iniquities separating us from the face of our God. There are many examples of the usage of this Hebrew word *badal* in the Word, and it means to separate or to divide something from another, whether physically or spiritually.

When we decree a thing, we use the Word of God to separate ourselves, our families, our health, etc. from the power of negative reports filled with danger, sickness, death, poverty, or any other form of the curse.

In Exodus 14:15-16, when God commands Moses to lift up his rod and stretch out his hand over the Red Sea and divide it, not only does He make a supernatural passageway for the Israelites to cross over, but He creates and decrees a divider of protection between them and harm's way of Pharaoh and his evil men pursuing them in verses 13-14:

> *And Moses said to the people, "Do not be afraid. Stand still, and see the salvation of the Lord, which He will accomplish for you today. For the Egyptians whom you see today, you shall see again no more forever. The Lord will fight for you, and you shall hold your peace."*

Let's look at a biblical example of a verbal decree to divide the godly from the ungodly. In Joshua 24:15, Joshua decrees over his family, *"...As for me and my house, we will serve the Lord."* Joshua verbally creates a divider, a spiritual boundary or wall between those who serve the Lord and those who don't. And He decrees that His family will serve God.

We separate ourselves from sickness and disease when we decree God's healing promise that *"by His stripes we are healed."* During a recent healing seminar in Ocala, Florida, a woman stepped forward for her healing. She had a bad fall that severely damaged seven of her discs, three in her neck and four in her lower back area, and the fall caused all of her nerves in her right shoulder to be pinched. She went to doctor, and received shots to help with the pain. She said the shots helped a little but not much. She could not lift her arm or bend over. And she struggled to sleep at night because of the pain. She was scheduled for neck, back, and shoulder surgery within a month, but something supernatural happened instead. She said she heard about the healing seminar for two weeks and made up her mind to attend.

That entire weekend she heard the healing word being decreed over her and everyone who attended the services.

Sunday morning she came forward, and I decreed that *"by His stripes you are healed."* I told her to put her faith into action and do what she was not able to do before. She started to move her neck, and she said her neck cracked about seven times, and those of us who were near her heard the last crack. It was so loud that the crowd all wowed at the same time. Instantly the woman was completely healed. She regained total movement in both her arms, she could bend and squat and do things she had not been able to do in a number of years—all because we believed and decreed and she aligned her faith to the healing decree and her physical healing manifested the moment she believed.

Decrees are based on the Word of God and produce in the physical realm what they are verbally sent out to do. Now let's use this spiritual principle of decreeing to help overcome chronic anxiety and depression and a spirit of fear.

Help to Overcome Chronic Anxiety and Depression

Chronic anxiety and depression are running rampant among people today, even throughout the Church. One of my readers wrote me with the following request, "Becky, I need help for healing from chronic anxiety and depression." I ask you now, you who hold this book in your hand, "Is this request too difficult for God?" You answer in your heart, "No." Then let me ask you another question, "Is chronic anxiety and depression too difficult for the Christian to overcome?" Many struggle with this type of inner healing, but I remind you again, *"With God..."* not in your own strength, but with Him, *all things are possible,* even this situation is possible to triumph over.

And just how do you win over this type of attack of destruction? You win with *God* and with the *power of the spoken word.*

In Jesus' name, that's correct, with our God, Jesus Christ, with the power of His name, you use the authority of your words and verbally renounce the spirit of fear and depression. Again, with your vocal chords you command these evil spirits out and off of you. You decree with your voice a radical turn around in the way you see and hear things, the way you respond to others and even to the past. Use this Scripture, *"For I will restore health to you and heal you of your wounds,' says the Lord"* (Jeremiah 30:17).

Decree God's Word to Overcome a Spirit of Fear

I decree that God has not given me a spirit of fear, but of power and of love and of a sound mind, Second Timothy 1:7. I am strong and courageous, I am not afraid, or dismayed, for the Lord my God is with me wherever I go, Joshua 1:9. I am established in righteousness, far from oppression, I will not fear; terror shall not come near me, Isaiah 54:14. The peace of God, which surpasses all understanding, guards my heart and mind through Christ Jesus, Philippians 4:7.

I set my mind on things above, not on things on the earth, Colossians 3:2. And whatever things are true, whatever things are noble, whatever things are just, whatever things are pure, whatever things are lovely, whatever things are of good report, if there is any virtue and if there is anything praiseworthy—I meditate on these things, Philippians 4:8.

I am strong and courageous, I am not afraid, or dismayed, for the Lord my God is with me wherever I go, Joshua 1:9. I am bold as a lion, Proverbs 28:1. I have the authority to trample on serpents and scorpions, and over all the power of the enemy, and nothing shall by any means hurt me, Luke 10:19.

The Lord is on my side; I will not fear. What can man do to me? Psalm 118:6. God is for me, so who can be against me? Romans 8:31. The Lord is my light and my salvation; whom shall I fear? The Lord is the strength of my life; of whom shall I be afraid? Psalm 27:1.

Peace I leave with you, My peace I give to you; not as the world gives do I give to you. Let not your heart be troubled, neither let it be afraid, John 14:27. Fear not, for I am with you; be not dismayed, for I am your God. I will strengthen you, yes, I will help you, I will uphold you with My righteous right hand, Isaiah 41:10.

Therefore, I do not worry about tomorrow, for tomorrow will worry about its own things. Sufficient for the day is its own trouble, Matthew 6:34. I cast all my care upon Him, for He cares for me, First Peter 5:7.

For I am persuaded that neither death nor life, nor angels nor principalities nor powers, nor things present nor things to come, nor height nor depth, nor any other created thing, shall be able to separate me from the love of God, which is in Christ Jesus my Lord, Romans 8:38-39.

I sought the Lord, and He heard me, and delivered me from all my fears, Psalm 34:4.

In Jesus' name I declare these promises of God over myself, amen.

This leads us into the next chapter, The Power of Your Supernatural Language, and how this spiritual weapon of warfare releases a little girl from a demonic stronghold, and how you can do much more with the gift of tongues.

Personal Word Checkup

Is this faith element of decreeing by faith new to me? If it's not new to me, have I been faithfully using this powerful element in my prayer life? Have I been decreeing things correctly? If not, do I understand this faith principle now? What is one thing that comes to my mind now that I should start to decree in my life immediately?

Group Discussion

As a group brainstorm together and decide on one thing in your area that you can use this element of faith and start to decree the Word of God over the situation.

Questions for Chapter 12—Decrees of Faith

1. What is the Hebrew word for "decree"? And what does it mean?

2. What are decrees are based upon? And what do they produce?

Note

1. Hebrew word definitions are provided by *Strong's Concordance* and can be found at Blue Letter Bible: https://www.blueletterbible.org.

Chapter 13

THE POWER OF YOUR
SUPERNATURAL LANGUAGE

Next to the blood and the name of Jesus and the Word of God, praying in supernatural languages has been the greatest gift given to us on this earth. It helps us in every area of life to overcome the problems of this life, the villainous attacks of the enemy, and thrust us into the supernatural realm of the Holy Spirit like no other. Let's talk a bit about the power of our supernatural language now.

By the leading of the Holy Spirit, our family felt compelled of the Lord to take in a sibling group of three girls. All abused by evil people, neglected and malnourished, shunned away from decency, and in great need of godly encouragement and affection. The eldest held her head down and with a nervous twitch constantly blinked her eyes with great fear of people; the middle child was severely neglected, lacked all sense of boundaries, and would leap unexpectedly into the arms of a stranger; and then there was the youngest, beautiful like her sisters, and very tiny and boney from a lack of proper nourishment. She appeared frail and weak but was possessed by a demon, and a stronghold of rebellion would suddenly manifest in the spur of a moment, anytime and anyplace.

One day was particularly strenuous and the demonic activity continued to manifest throughout the entire day. Challenging us in everything and anything, and for nothing. Finally, I held the youngest little girl and hugged her tightly and began to pray quietly in my supernatural, heavenly language. And as I released prophetic deliverance and healing into this girl, the demon within her began to squirm and fight me. I continued with increased fervor until I physically felt the release and this precious one melted in my arms.

She held me tightly and from that moment of prophetic deliverance the process of prophetic healing fueled by the power of loved-filled words began to crack her hardened heart, and she took comfort, as they all did as I released prophetic healing through this glorious gift of praying in tongues.

Along with the power to deliver someone from demonic oppression and possession, praying in tongues helps you to break the unruliness of your tongue. It helps to bring it under submission to God, like the example of the wild horse mentioned in Chapter 2, under the subtitle, Right Words Bridle the Whole Body.

Is Tongues of the Devil?

Is praying or speaking in tongues of the devil? Here is what the Bible has to say about it: *"And these signs will follow those who believe: In My name they will cast out demons; they will speak with new tongues"* (Mark 16:17). No, it is not of the devil. The Bible says if we believe, we ourselves will speak with new tongues.

Edify Yourself

The Bible also teaches us about the power of speaking in tongues. We read in First Corinthians 14:4, *"He who speaks in a tongue edifies himself...."* When we speak in our supernatural language, we encourage and build ourselves up in the power of the Holy Spirit. We can break off a spirit of depression, worry, anxiety, and fear when we edify ourselves in the Holy Spirit and pray in tongues.

The girls we have taken in to live with our family all come with such an unnatural fear of everything. I am speaking of the paralyzing type of fear that often makes no sense in the natural, and it can't make human sense because it is a demon of fear.

As I write, we are at the beach this week for a family vacation of soaking in the sun and swimming and playing at the beach—and two of the three girls are petrified of the ocean. They took one look at it and began to scream and run in sheer terror. This puts quite a damper on a beach vacation.

So, we rolled up our sleeves, so to speak, and began to pray in tongues, and all their fears about the ocean are gone, and they enjoy it as much as we do.

Praying in tongues is designed to build you up, to overcome—just like the girls went from paralyzing fear to not fearing at all, and actually having the time of their lives.

Get back to edifying yourself and pray in tongues starting today.

How Does the Holy Spirit Help Us Pray?

Romans 8:26-27 informs us how the Holy Spirit helps us when we do not know how to pray:

> *Likewise the Spirit also helps in our weaknesses. For we do not know what we should pray for as we ought, but the Spirit Himself makes intercession for us with groanings which cannot be uttered. Now He who searches the hearts knows what the mind of the Spirit is, because He makes intercession for the saints according to the will of God.*

Rules about Praying and Speaking in Tongues

So that we do things decent and in order, let's talk about some rules about how to pray and speak in tongues. First things first, to receive the baptism of the Holy Spirit there is only one requirement to meet—you must be born again.

And no one puts new wine into old wineskins; or else the new wine will burst the wineskins and be spilled, and the wineskins will be ruined. But the new wine must be put into new wineskins, and both are preserved (Luke 5:37-38).

Only a recreated spirit by the blood of Jesus can house the power of the Holy Spirit. This power of God would utterly destroy an unbeliever. If you are born again, you can receive this powerful language of the Holy Spirit.

When we pray in tongues by ourselves, we do not need to have the message interpreted. God is not the author of confusion, but of order and peace; so when we speak in tongues in a public meeting, we need to have the tongue interpreted so what is said can be understood by the people.

If anyone speaks in a tongue, let there be two or at the most three, each in turn, and let one interpret. But if there is no interpreter, let him keep silent in church, and let him speak to himself and to God (1 Corinthians 14:27-28).

Pray that You May Interpret the Message of the Tongue

"Therefore let him who speaks in a tongue pray that he may interpret" (1 Corinthians 14:13). Since May 1979, I have been born again and baptized in the power of the Holy Spirit with the evidence of praying and speaking in tongues at the same time. I have also received the interpretation of the message of the tongue. This is biblical. God clearly wants you to understand the mysteries that you are praying or speaking. *"For he who speaks in a tongue does not speak to men but to God, for no one understands him; however, in the spirit he speaks mysteries"* (1 Corinthians 14:2). When we use this spiritual gift of tongues, we speak directly to the Spirit of God, and in mysteries. This is why we need to pray that we may interpret the tongues.

I have been blessed in that after I became born again, every time the doors of the meeting place were open I was there and I sat under Holy Spirit-inspired messages from the Word. It was here I was trained not to be religious, but to have relationship with God. I spent much alone time with God from the beginning of my new birth, and the Word of God not only cleansed me, it equipped me in the spirit realm as well. I could not get enough of the Word or of the Spirit. Prior to this time in my life, I had been raised in a denominational church that didn't teach us we needed to be born again or anything about the Holy Spirit and the power He gave us to overcome. So when I gave my life to Christ and received the baptism of the Holy Spirit, I had no reservations about the Spirit of God, I was unchurched or unlearned when it came to Him. I was not filled with a bunch of religious rules. I learned directly from the Spirit how to flow in His ways. My heart was so pliable and tender toward Him. I would spend hours in the Word and then pray in tongues; and from my beginning with Him, the interpretation of the tongues would flow out of my mouth in English and I have been blessed with a rich relationship with Him because of these things. I have had real intimate communication with Holy Spirit since the day I became born again and baptized in the Holy Spirit with the evidence of praying in tongues.

I remember as a new believer I shared in a small Bible study I was part of about these deep conversations I would have with the Lord while praying in tongues. We were all new believers in this group and they would question the validity of what I would share. One who was of a very religious spirit would try to talk me out of these things. But I knew the person did not understand, because this individual did not walk in the level of relationship with the Spirit that I had.

All the hours of praying in the Spirit, or in tongues, brought forth healing and deliverance that I so needed as I had been living in the world before then. And the mysteries He would reveal to me by the way of interpretation always came to pass. Don't allow others who have not developed their prayer language to talk you out of the deep riches God has for you with this spiritual language. I would not be where I am today without the vocabulary of the Holy Spirit.

So during healing services, seminars, and conferences, I often give a prophecy that starts by the gift of speaking in tongues, but the Spirit always gives me the interpretation for the people as well. Why? Because I ask Him for the interpretation and I desire that the people hear from the Lord, not just from me. And while ministering healing to the sick, I often pray in tongues and this is when I receive the interpretation in visual form and will see into the Spirit realm and see the condition of the heart of the person—what may be hindering the healing from manifesting, what is the root cause of the problem, and/or have a message from the Lord for the individual as well.

Paul cautions us not to use the excuse to prophesy in tongues as an excuse to forbid to speak in tongues in public. *"Therefore, brethren, desire earnestly to prophesy, and do not forbid to speak with tongues"* (1 Corinthians 14:39).

Paul encourages us to pray in tongues: *"praying always with all prayer and supplication in the Spirit, being watchful to this end with all perseverance and supplication for all the saints"* (Ephesians 6:18).

Jude also exhorts us to pray in tongues, *"But you, beloved, building yourselves up on your most holy faith, praying in the Holy Spirit"* (Jude 1:20).

Our faith is now stirred to begin or to continue to pray in faith with our supernatural languages to release prophetic and healing power into our every need and situation in the name of Jesus for His glory. Now, let's stir our faith in the amazing prophetic gift of the Word of Knowledge.

Personal Word Checkup

Am I born again? Am I baptized in the power of the Holy Spirit? Do I pray and speak in tongues? Do I pray often in my heavenly language?

Group Discussion

Leaders, be ready to minister the baptism of the Holy Spirit to those in your group who have not received the baptism as of yet. Together as a group pray in your supernatural language. Pray that you would interpret the tongue as well.

Questions for Chapter 13—The Power of Your Supernatural Language

1. According to Mark 16:17, what does the Bible say if we believe?

2. First Corinthians 4:4 tells us what we do when we pray in tongues, what is it?

3. What is the one thing that can house the power of the Holy Spirit?

4. According to Romans 8:26-27, how does the Holy Spirit help us?

5. In this portion of Scripture, how does the Holy Spirit help us when we do not know how to pray?

6. First Corinthians 14:13 tells us that there is something we should do when we pray in tongues. What is it?

7. First Corinthians 14:2 tells us that when we speak in tongues we speak to someone. Who is it?

8. According to this Scripture verse, what do we speak when we speak in tongues?

9. Paul cautions us in First Corinthians 14:39 that we should not use the excuse to prophesy in tongues as an excuse to what?

10. How does Paul encourage us to pray in Ephesians 6:18?

11. According to Paul in Ephesians 6:18, how are we to make supplication?

12. How does Jude exhort us to pray in the Spirit in Jude 1:20?

CHAPTER 14

WORD OF KNOWLEDGE

One of the gifts of the Holy Spirit mentioned in First Corinthians 12:8 is the word of knowledge: *"…to another the word of knowledge through the same Spirit."* What is this supernatural prophetic gift? The gift of the word of knowledge refers to the ability to know facts about a situation that are happening in the present tense, there is no future telling in the word of knowledge. You would not otherwise have knowledge of the situation, but for the spiritual insight of the Holy Spirit.

This is a powerful gift that empowers someone to minister into the lives of people. And it also helps the receivers know that God hears and cares for their needs. To unbelievers it is a sign that Jesus Christ is real, and it opens up their hearts to receive the message God has prepared for them. It also gives the one ministering, whether from the pulpit or in an everyday situation, detailed direction as to how the Lord would have the person minister.

Debilitating Back Pain Healed

I was in Lexington, Virginia, and was about to minister at a meeting. The Lord gave me a word of knowledge that someone in the meeting was suffering from back pain and that the pain was deep within the body. I did not know that the host of this meeting was the one this word of knowledge was for. He did not let on to me that he was suffering and had to sleep that afternoon because of the debilitating pain. When I delivered the word of knowledge, the man stood up because he knew God heard and cared for his physical need for healing. I released the healing power of the Holy Spirit into the man and asked him to do what he was unable to do before, and he was instantly healed. This is how words of knowledge operate. It's a form of communication from the Holy Spirit delivered to one person for another.

Other Ways a Word of Knowledge Operates

So that you can understand what I am writing about, I will give you a few examples of how I have received words of knowledge. I was ministering healing to people at the end of a healing service. I came to one woman, and I could see in a vision a mature forest of trees (the Lord uses images of trees and their condition to reveal to me the condition of the hearts of the people I am ministering to), and in the midst of this forest was a fallen dead log that had moss growing all over it. I knew in my spirit that this woman was spiritually dead, even though she was a regular churchgoer. Before I could minister healing, she needed to make a decision to receive Jesus as her Savior.

I was ministering healing to a young man on his deathbed, and I began to see a tall, mature oak tree that was full of leaves in fall colors and the leaves were falling from the tree. I knew that this young man was healed from the cancer that was attacking his body and that he would live to be a healthy, old man.

I was praying one morning before I started to minister to a group of pastors. As I was praying in the Spirit, I began to see into the realm of the supernatural. I was standing on the shore of a beautiful crystal-clear lake. As I was looking into the water, something started forming in the water and all of a sudden a large snake came right up to me out of the water and looked me in the eye. I knew that there were false preachers and teachers in this group of pastors and that there was also witchcraft being practiced by someone in this group. And it was all true.

Along with trees, the Spirit shows me the spiritual condition of the receiver with scenes of water. The condition of the water shows me the state of their heart. If the water is dirty or muddy, I know there is a lot of sin issues in their lives. If the water is stagnant, so too is their spiritual walk with the Lord. If the water is crystal clear, they are pure in heart before God. If the water is rough, they are passing through difficult times. If the water is smooth, they are at peace with the Lord.

He also uses the word of knowledge in numerous ways to help me minister to a crowd of people with accuracy. He will give me a list of ailments among the crowd and before I start to minister the message, I will first read this list of sicknesses, diseases, and other situations to the people. I have found these lists to be spot-on. Even when these things appear to be bazaar to me, they always minister directly to the people. I no longer question these words of knowledge, I just speak them out as they come to me.

I will often feel the finger of God press on different body parts and I will write these things down on a sheet of paper. Mixed into this word of knowledge that the Spirit wants me to know about the crowd, I will hear Him say a name of a disease or a sin issue. I will also see words in my mind's eye and I add them to my list. This prophetic list is always right on and it builds the faith of the people to receive their miracle.

These are just some of the ways that Holy Spirit prophetically reveals to me through a word of knowledge what I need to know about the individual or crowd to whom I am ministering healing.

Personal Word Checkup

Have I ever received a word of knowledge from someone concerning a physical healing I was believing God for? If so, did I activate my faith and receive my healing? Am I open to this form of communication with the Holy Spirit and His people?

Group Discussion

Talk about this supernatural gift of the Holy Spirit. Enter into a time of prayer and wait upon the Lord to see if this is the way His Spirit will speak to you.

Questions for Chapter 14—Word of Knowledge

1. What is the word of knowledge?

2. Where in the Word is it mentioned as a gift of the Holy Spirit?

3. What's one way this powerful gift empowers someone?

4. How does this gift help the receiver?

5. How does this gift help an unbeliever?

6. How does this gift help the one ministering, whether from the pulpit or in an everyday situation?

CHAPTER 15

CALL THINGS INTO BEING

Calling things into being is addressed in Romans 4:17, *"(as it is written, "I have made you a father of many nations") in the presence of Him whom he believed—God, who gives life to the dead and calls those things which do not exist as though they did."* Again, this is another confirmation that God has placed the responsibility to heal with us.

It is important that we understand this prophetic power that is in our words to heal and to speak things into existence with faith-filled words. We are the ones who are to do this, God's not going to do this for us. We will do it for ourselves—by His authority that He gave to us.

What I am going to write here may be new and different for you, but my goal is to teach you how to speak with the authority Christ gave you, and with the power of the Holy Spirit to achieve the results you so desire and that God desires even more for you.

Ask yourself, *How do I ask God to create or recreate specific body parts?*

Number one, according to the Word, right before Jesus gave up His Spirit He cried out, *"It is finished"* (John 19:30). Every sickness and disease, named or unnamed, known or unknown, every form of the curse was dealt with and paid for by the blood of Jesus. Isaiah 53:4-5 declares that *"by His stripes"* we have already been healed. He took upon His own body every illness and every pain. This is our base to move forward with clarity in the answer to this question.

You wonder, *How do I ask God to create or recreate my body parts?* Jesus already worked the ill-stricken, weakened, or dead body part out of your body at the whipping post, purchased your creative miracle with His blood, then released resurrection power when He rose from the grave, and then gave to you the Holy Spirit, and all authority over satan and his wicked works—because of all this, you do not ask God to create or to recreate body parts. He gave you this responsibility and empowered you with the supernatural *dunamus* power of the Spirit to accomplish the impossible.

Jesus cleared the path for you to tap into this explosive miracle-working ability with the power of your words. You are to deactivate the deadly acts of satan against your body and activate Jehovah Rapha's life-giving power and create or recreate what you have need of for yourself, by the correct usage of your spoken words.

You want further explanation of what I say here? One day before I traveled back home from a ministry trip to Tanzania, East Africa, I stepped off the bus and let out a cry of pain as my knee began to rub bone-on-bone. It was extremely painful and difficult to walk with. But I claimed immediate authority over the situation, and from that point on I did not cry, whimper, or complain. I exercised the covenant power of the spoken word that I have with the Father. Even though I did not know what had happened to my knee, I began to prophesy over it, "In Jesus' name, my knee is healed." When I arrived in Guatemala, my husband asked me, "Was that your knee I just heard?" In response to his concern I replied, "My knee is just fine, thank you. By His stripes, my knee is healed." And he knew not to question, but to align his faith with mine.

And I continued using the supernatural creative vocabulary of the Holy Spirit: "My knee is recreated in the name of Jesus." And in spite of every pain-filled step, I would only speak words that heal, "I walk, I run, I dance, I squat, I kneel with no pain in the name of the Lord." I spoke creatively according to my need with law of the spoken word, "In Jesus' name, I have the right amount of cartilage in my knee, and it bends with ease." And to the glory of God and for my good pleasure, within two or three days my knee was pain-free, and it could do what it was created and recreated to do—bend with ease.

And this principle of calling things that do not exist as though they already did was how we recreated dead body parts for our son, Marcos, whom we not only raised from the dead, but spoke new body parts into existence, like a new heart, lungs, kidneys, and a new brain. And the same again for another of our adopted sons, Andres, who no longer is autistic. This faith principle works—call things into existence by faith in the redemptive blood of Jesus Christ.

Prophesy to Specific Body Parts

Jesus, by His own free will, knelt down at the whipping post and suffered and bled deep and painful whippings in our stead so that we can now be delivered and healed from all forms of pain, sickness, and disease.

With the healing power of this revelation, take on the spirit of prophecy and prophesy to your bones and to every part of your body. Renounce death and speak life into your mortal body. Recreate broken and worn-out body parts with faith-filled words. Learn to prophesy life instead of death, and healing in place of sickness.

It is not as difficult as you fear because Jesus was crowned with the crown of thorns, He became the curse for you. Why? So you can be free from it. But like you've been learning, your healing starts with your spoken words. Come on now, be bold and release the power of prophetic words and unleash that creative miracle you seek.

And remember, while you are prophesying to your specific body parts, I encourage you to utilize the other elements of faith that we have been studying too.

Brain Tumor—Gone!

A woman from Europe writes to me with an urgent prayer request. The following are exchanges between the two of us:

Dear Becky,

Please pray for me. I am under attack from the enemy. I just returned from a mission's trip to Africa the other day. I woke up in the morning and the right side of my head started to swell. I went to the doctor and had my head scanned. Today I went for the results and the doctor said I have a tumor in my brain. I immediately cancelled the negative report in the name of Jesus. I have to go for a MRI tomorrow at 8 A.M. Please join your faith with me that the tumor is gone in the name of Jesus.

Dear Sister-in-Jesus,

I renounce this curse and assignment against you. There is no tumor that can stand against the blood of Jesus. I release the power of His blood over you, and declare that by His healing stripes you are healed. No matter what the MRI shows or does not show, the Word of God is firm and you are healed in Jesus' name, amen.

Dear Becky,

Amen and amen, I receive this in Jesus' name.

Dear Sister-in-Jesus,

I wrote this short blog post last night with you in mind. Remember, I am standing with you for your complete healing in Jesus' name.

Speak the Scriptures Aloud and Live

The battle is raging; in the natural the odds are not in your favor, but does this mean you are defeated? No, it does not. Now is not the time to give up, but the time to pick up the Sword of the Spirit and wield it in your favor. *"And take the helmet of salvation, and the sword of the Spirit, which is the word of God"* (Eph. 6:17). The Sword of the Spirit is the spoken word of God. And you have to take up the Scriptures and speak them aloud until they produce what you have need of.

Do you allow satan the last word in a battle? If so, don't. Words have the power to produce life or death. It's important to override the enemy's report of defeat and death with words of faith, life, and victory. *"Death and life are in the power of the tongue, and they that love it shall eat the fruit thereof"* (Prov. 18:21).

If you receive a bad medical report filled with death and doom, override it with spoken words of faith. Say aloud, *"I shall not die, but live, and declare the works of the Lord"* (Ps. 118:17).

If they say, "There is no hope." You turn the situation around and speak forth, *"Then I am in right standing for a miracle. According to Matthew 19:26, "With men this is impossible, but with God all things are possible."*

Is this craziness? No, it's faith talk, and it is pleasing to the Father. And if you will work it, it will produce life and healing every time. But you must be consistent. And only speak God's healing promises over yourself. Do not speak about the death report. Speak God's report that decrees, *"But if the Spirit of Him who raised Jesus from the dead dwells in you, He who raised Christ from the dead will also give life to your mortal bodies through His Spirit who dwells in you"* (Rom. 8:11).

The vocabulary of faith defies the natural realm of understanding. And it is a supernatural weapon given to us to use for God's glory in our lives. And if and when we do wield this weapon of faith and decree life in place of death, healing instead of sickness, and strength over weakness the manifestation of our much desired miracle will manifest.

Dear Becky,

Praise the Lord! Thank you so much for these words of encouragement. I proclaimed them throughout the whole day yesterday.

Jesus changed the pictures of last week's CT and it surprised the doctors yesterday at the hospital. What they saw in the

MRI is different from the CT, and they have never seen anything like this before. The tumor melted into liquid! They gave me an antibiotic and sent me home.

Glory and honor to Jesus, amen!

Yes, glory to God indeed! We have the power of life and death in the tongue, and those of us who will activate this supernatural power and speak forth prophetic healing power will enjoy the fruit this miracle-working power produces.

What did this woman need? She needed a healthy brain, one that was free from tumors, pain, and swelling. She created the very thing she needed by calling forth those things that were not as though they already were.

What do you have need of? Are you willing to do as this woman did and activate the prophetic and healing power of your words and call into being things that are not as though they already were?

Prophetic Proclamations for a Healthy Brain

I believe with God all things are possible, even healing from memory loss and serious brain traumas. There is no limit what we can access in the realm of the Holy Spirit when it comes to healing and recreation of sick and dead body parts. Let's create a few prophetic proclamations to prophesy for a healthy brain.

Memory Care

Now I know you will agree with me that this is a serious problem and the enemy uses the weapon of memory loss to inflict suffering upon people. But do we have to settle for less than God's best? Do we have to accept these attacks as a normal part of aging? Can we trust God for recreated brain cells when they are injured or depleted from the curse of this fallen world?

Instead of saying, "I can't remember what I'm doing next." Simply speak aloud, "I can remember what I am doing, because I have the mind of Christ." And as I have already taught you in this work, if you are consistent with your words, your body, in this case your memory, will submit and surrender to the words you speak.

When you are frustrated and tempted to say, "I can't figure this out," reverse the negative to God's positive realm of faith and prophesy over your memory, "I can do all things through Christ who strengthens me." And add the healing touch to this prophetic proclamation, "I can do all things, even heal in my brain and in my mind and emotions, through Christ who strengthens me." This means you have a choice in your health care. Either you can submit yourself to satan's nasty attacks against your memory, or you can get in line with God's Word and His ways and regain your memory. This is refreshing news.

If you struggle with word recall, prophesy over yourself, "Because I activate the Word of God in my life, I prophesy that I do have perfect word recall. I can remember names and what I want to say next." Work this faith principle until you see the results, and then keep your lips from cursing your word recall.

Confusion

When passing through difficult times and suffering from a state of confusion, claim hold of your healing in Jesus and speak out loud, "I renounce a spirit of confusion. I release the Spirit of Peace and I prophesy that this supernatural fog has lifted, and I understand clearly now in Jesus' name." If you desire clarity of mind, then start to operate in the power of the tongue to produce this clarity.

Brain Functions

For abnormalities of the brain, prophesy this over yourself or tweak it with the proper pronouns for a loved one, "My right side of the brain is recreated and my left side responds accordingly. And my left side of the brain is also recreated, and the functions on my right side operate correctly."

For overall brain functions, prophesy over yourself, "I have the mind of Christ and my faculties are up to speed."

Epilepsy

Instead of settling for less than God's creative intentions for you, activate your authority in the name of Jesus and declare, "In Jesus' name, I renounce an epileptic spirit, and these seizures must stop! The pathways in my brain that have been dug via these seizures have been erased by the blood of Jesus, and they cannot be reopened, and new seizure pathways cannot be made, because I am delivered and healed and possess the mind of Christ."

You doubt this? You still struggle to believe that your words can control your state-of-being? It is the will and the doing of Elohim that gives us prophetic power in our words to do His bidding—heal the sick in His name. Remember, you are created in the likeness of the Father and possess supernatural power in your words. It is also the will of the Father that all of His sons and daughters are created in the mirror image of His Son, Yeshua, and as He is so are you on this earth and you represent His redemptive qualities.

It is also the will of the Trinity of God that you are endowed with the creative, explosive power of the Holy Spirit to move in the realm of the miraculous. You have been given authority to have dominion on this earth; and in the name of Jesus, you are to subdue the earth, this includes all works of the enemy. And sickness and disease are part of his wicked works.

Over and over again I see this work. Why? Because I believe God's message that we have prophetic and healing power in our words. Will you trust and believe God and activate His power He gave to you?

Now, let's brainstorm and come up with a plan of action to create an atmosphere of healing with your words in the next chapter.

Personal Word Checkup

Have I been calling out to God to heal me? Do I now see that He already has healed me and now it is my responsibility to activate my healing with my prophetic words? Is there something that I need healing for? What words can I start to prophesy over myself for my healing to manifest?

Group Discussion

With your group discuss how to call things that are not into being. Together do so for one another's needs. Depending upon the size of your group this may be best to do in small groups of two or three people.

Questions for Chapter 15—Call Things into Being

1. When was every sickness and disease, named or unnamed, known or unknown, every form of the curse dealt with and paid for by the blood of Jesus?

2. According to Isaiah 53:4-5, what did Jesus already do for us?

3. How were we healed?

4. What type of power has He given to us to create with?

5. Jesus cleared the path for you to tap into this explosive miracle working power with what power?

6. What am I to do with the power of these words?

PART THREE

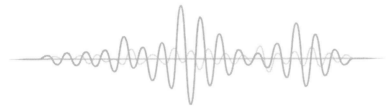

A PLAN OF ACTION

CHAPTER 16

CREATE AN ATMOSPHERE OF HEALING WITH YOUR WORDS

Word of the Lord

You've been crying out to Me for help. I've sent you My Word, and I now I send you a plan of action to implement My Word in your situation. If you will work My Word to the letter, you will have success in all that you work it for, thus sayeth the Lord, Your Healer.

Seek and Surround Yourself with Great Faith

Do you need a miracle? Then it's of utmost importance to seek out and surround yourself with people of faith. People who are not ashamed to speak the faith language, and certainly people who live like they truly do believe. Why? According to First Corinthians 15:33, we are warned about the people with whom we keep company. It clearly states, *"Do not be deceived, 'Evil company corrupts good habits.'"* This word "corrupts" in Greek is *phtheirō*, and it means to defile, destroy, deprave (Strong's G5351). This draws a very clear picture of what happens to our habits of faith when we do not align ourselves correctly with others of strong faith. Think about this for a while.

When you align yourself with people of weak faith or people who are ignorant of the supernatural power of faith, you allow them to defile your faith. The Merriam-Webster online dictionary definition of "defile" is to make impure or unclean. It also means to contaminate, which implies intrusion of or contact with dirt or foulness from an outside source. It describes "deprave" as to pervert or to pollute, and it describes "destroy" as to put an end to the existence of (something) by damaging or attacking it.

It's worth the effort to search the real meaning of the words used in the Bible, and in this case you can see the seriousness of choosing the company you keep. The last thing you need when activating your faith for a miracle is to be surrounded by unbelieving people, including unbelieving believers. These types of people will put an end to the existence of your miracle by damaging or attacking your faith. They will contaminate your faith, make it impure or unclean, with their doubt. You cannot afford to pollute your faith with their unbelief.

What did Jesus do when He encountered a room full of doubt? He kicked them out. He did not allow them to contaminate the spiritual atmosphere with their unbelief. Let's read this testimony from Luke 8:50-55:

> But when Jesus heard it, He answered him, saying, "Do not be afraid; only believe, and she will be made well." When He came into the house, He permitted no one to go in except Peter, James, and John, and the father and mother of the girl. Now all wept and mourned for her; but He said, "Do not weep; she is not dead, but sleeping." And they ridiculed Him, knowing that she was dead. But He put them all outside, took her by the hand and called, saying, "Little girl, arise." Then her spirit returned, and she arose immediately. And He commanded that she be given something to eat.

Do you see the reason to seek and surround yourself with people of strong faith when you are in need of a miracle? Jesus was about to raise Jairus' daughter from the dead, but the unbelievers in the power of doubt ridiculed Him when He declared by faith that she was not dead, just asleep.

The power of the spoken word rising against the resurrection of this girl would literally bury her. He knew the atmosphere of faith for this girl's life had to be cleansed from the destructive power of doubt-filled words being activated from the people. The vocabulary of death with all their wailing, moaning, and groaning had to be evicted from the spiritual realm of the miraculous. He made them leave so that the only supernatural force activated in that room was faith, and it overpowered the spirit of death, released the Spirit of Life, and the girl came back to life.

This is exactly what we had to do when we raised our son, Marcos, from the dead. We had to purify the spiritual atmosphere from all doubt and unbelief so that the supernatural power of our faith could override the spirit of death with the Spirit of Life, and he came back to life; and dead body parts were recreated for the glory of the Lord and for our good pleasure of the completion of our family.

And allow me to mention now that you may have to look outside of your local church fellowship to find people who will stand in faith and believe with you for your miracle.

CHAPTER 17

BUILD A SUPPORT TEAM
THAT WORKS

I've taught you from the beginning in my first work, *DARE to Believe,* how to create a support team based upon the teachings in the Bible involving Joshua, Moses, Aaron and Hur, and the Amalekites.

To refresh your memory, Joshua was fighting against the enemy, the Amalekites. But he was not alone in this battle, upholding Joshua was Moses on the mountaintop with his arms raised up. When Moses would grow weary his arms would fall down and the enemy would overpower Joshua. But then two more men of God came into play, Aaron and Hur. They climbed to the mountaintop to support Moses, raising up his arms and holding them there. And as they supported Moses, Joshua would gain and eventually won the battle against the enemy.

This discovery came to me when someone asked me if I knew of a Scripture reference for someone who received support for supporting another. I told the person that I believed that was scriptural; and when I found it in the Bible I would share it with her. And my studies led me to Exodus 17.

How does this apply to us? I believe this is God's model for us of a support team that actually works. Let's discuss who is who in this team before we start to form our support team.

Joshua represents the person fighting on the frontlines. The person who is fighting against sickness, disease, and death. Moses is the main support for the Joshua. Usually this is the one or ones closest to the person who is actually in the midst of the raging battle—like a spouse, parents, a sibling, or best friend. The Aaron and the Hur are those who see that Moses is growing weary and come up to the mountaintop and lift up and hold up the arms of Moses. They are Moses' personal support group.

Now, some people want to fill the shoes of the members of the group, they want to be the all in all, but that's not God's best in the situation. And I understand that not all Christians have been prepared to properly support those in a battle against death. I believe they want to be, but don't know how. They lack proper teaching and training to fill the shoes of any one of these biblical characters. But this scenario is about to change, and for the better.

Forming Your Support Team

It is of utmost importance that you form a support team that is in 100 percent agreement with God's promises to heal in spirit, soul, and in physical body. You will be operating in all of the faith elements and prayer strategies discussed in this work. Now let's get to work and form this team.

Ask yourself the following questions and be honest with your answers.

1. Who do I know who is a born-again believer in Jesus Christ?
2. Who do I know that is born again and is baptized in the Holy Spirit (this is not water baptism), and prays in tongues?
3. Who do I know who is born again and also believes in the healing power of the Lord?
4. Who do I know who believes that it is God's will to heal all people from all sickness and disease?
5. Is there anyone on my list who believes that God only heals some people, not all people?

6.   Is there anyone on my list who believes that God puts sickness and disease on people?

7.   Is anyone on this list that I am forming known to be a gossip?

8.   Is anyone on this list being formed known for their positive and encouraging attitude?

9.   Is there someone on my list who I know is dabbling in New Age doctrine? Or am I sure that everyone I have written down are fully committed to Jesus and the Bible?

10. Is there a born-again, Spirit-filled, tongue-talking pastor, deacon, or church leader in my area who believes 100 percent in the healing power of the Holy Spirit whom I can ask to be part of my support team?

11. If there is not a mature pastor, deacon or church leader as described in question 10, do I know of a mature couple or individual who fits the description that I could ask to join this team?

The purpose of this list of questions is to help you form a strong chain of believers. No weak link is allowed on this support team. You will pass through very trying times, and you cannot afford to have someone who is weak in the faith and will cause others to fail in their faith to believe with you or for your loved one's miracle to manifest.

In your support team, you must have individuals who are born-again believers in Jesus, they must be baptized in the Holy Spirit and pray in tongues. If they are born again but not baptized in the Holy Spirit and pray in tongues, are they willing to do so? If not, you cannot afford to have them on your support team. The members of this team must be aligned with the *dunamus* miracle-working power of the Holy Spirit in order for the miraculous to manifest.

Your team will suffer if you allow gossipers to be a part. Gossipers are not to be trusted to be a member of this team. They are immature in the faith, loose lipped with their words, and stir up trouble. Their sinful mouths will be the downfall of the team and the person you are teaming up for will die.

And only people who believe that God wills and is able to heal all people from all sickness and disease are allowed to be on your support team. Anyone who believes God puts sickness and disease upon people or that He only heals some people sometime is a weak link and will break the power of the chain of faith.

Use wisdom in choosing the members of this support team.

It would be wise for pastors to bring this teaching into their fellowships and actually train their members how to stand in faith and believe rightly for others in need of healing and miracles. And start to form support groups for those in need.

Why Is It Important that We Are in 100 Percent Agreement to Form the Team?

We cannot be doubleminded, either people believe or they don't believe in God's healing power for today. If one believes and another doesn't, then you have division and every wicked thing has access into the situation. All members must be on board 100 percent to be in agreement. The Bible teaches us that a house divided against itself cannot stand, well neither can a support group.

Beware Your Traditions Don't Interfere with God's Healing Power

Mark 7:13 warns us of the negative effects that traditions have against the word of God, *"Making the word of God of no effect through your tradition which you have handed down. And many such things you do."*

Beware of spiritual traditions that can stop the miraculous Word of God from creating the miracle you desire. I share in great detail the miraculous resurrection and healing of our son, Marcos, from the dead in my first work, *DARE to Believe,* in Chapter 11, pages 175-193. What I want to focus on here concerning his testimony is the power of man's tradition and how it kept interfering with the completion of Marcos' healing.

The interference we had to fight against was the tradition of the priests and nuns who made their everyday rounds in the hospital. When they came to Marcos, they daily performed their spiritual rituals for what they believed to be his death.

Every day we had to fight off the power of death of these rituals and words, saying, "In Jesus' name we renounce the spirit of death, and we release the Spirit of Life, we release the healing power of the Holy Spirit to flow in and throughout your entire body, in Jesus' holy name. You will live, and not die. You will fulfill your destiny, in Jesus' name."

Whose Words Are You Listening To?

It is important that you guard your heart from the unbelief of others. And I will add to this that you must discern spiritually who or what is standing before you. Again, I share in Marcos' dramatic testimony of how satan appeared to me as a doctor, and even had his medical file in his hand, and started to bombard me with negative predictions the day we were to bring him home from a very tough, but victorious battle. I share this, as often I hear people say that angels have been disguised in human form such as pastors, loved ones who had previously passed on from this world, medical personnel, angels of light, even in the form of butterflies. The list goes on and on as to what or who demons will disguise themselves. And their message is always along the line of doubt and defeat: "God says He is not going to heal you now. It's time to give up, let go, and come home."

You need to be super discerning during this battle. Quite frankly, God is not going to send His messengers, His angels, to deliver a message that goes against His healing Word. He never goes against the words written in the Bible. And what does His healing promise tell us? He bore our griefs, carried our sorrows and pains, was wounded for our transgressions, crushed for our wickedness, the punishment for our well-being fell upon Him, and by His wounds we are healed (see Isaiah 53:4-5).

My point is this, according to the healing Scriptures, which are many, you have already been healed. The enemy is delivering a false message and his camp is getting really worried because your miracle is about to manifest. This is why they are sending demons in disguise with discouraging messages. They are terrified of your healing testimony and the people who will be won over to the Kingdom of God. And they are afraid of the spiritual multiplication principle (see Genesis 1:26-28) that takes place when you take the Kingdom of God by force and fight the enemy until the promise of God manifests into the physical realm.

And while we are on this topic, you need to be smart as to what Scriptures you align yourself with during this period of healing. Make sure you align yourself with the Scriptures after Jesus redeems humankind from the curse.

An example of this principle: God put leprosy upon Miriam for speaking against her brother Moses for marrying an Ethiopian woman (you can read this account in Numbers 12:1-16). We need to understand that during the Old Testament times they were living under the curse of the law. And Miriam was punished for seven days with this disease. But since then, in the New Testament times, Jesus shed His blood to redeem us from the curse when He was crowned with the crown of thorns, see John 19:2, and as He completes the work of our redemption upon the cross. We are no longer under the letter of the law, but that of grace, and we've been redeemed from all forms of the curse, including sickness and disease. Jesus took upon His Body our punishment for our sins.

> *Christ has redeemed us from the curse of the law, having become a curse for us (for it is written, "Cursed is everyone who hangs on a tree") (Galatians 3:13).*

> *Surely He has borne our griefs and carried our sorrows; yet we esteemed Him stricken, smitten by God, and afflicted. But He was wounded for our transgressions, He was bruised for our*

iniquities; the chastisement for our peace was upon Him, and by His stripes we are healed" (Isaiah 53:4-5).

Lift Up the Healer, Not the Sickness

So many of God's people have this backward. Instead of lifting up the name of their Healer, Yeshua, they exalt the name of the sickness or disease that the enemy, satan, is using to destroy them with. Philippians 2:9-11 clearly says:

Therefore God highly exalted Him and gave Him the name which is above every name, that at the name of Jesus every knee should bow, of those in heaven and on earth and under the earth, and every tongue should confess that Jesus Christ is Lord, to the glory of God the Father.

The name of Jesus is higher than cancer, diabetes, Lyme disease, HIV, and all other disease, yet God's people continue to declare how powerful these wicked weapons of spiritual warfare are and deny the highest power of the greatest One, Jesus the Messiah.

Listening in on some conversations of Christians, one would surmise that Jesus is the lesser power, powerless or even worse, careless toward His followers; when in reality, He is Jehovah Rapha, the God who heals disease.

If God's people would truly humble themselves and bow before their Creator, they would come into the presence of His greatness and know firsthand the wonder of His name and the power behind His name.

All creation, including that which is in a fallen state, must bow before Jesus Christ. Sickness and disease are microscopic organisms that get into the human body and make people ill; but when put in their rightful place, they too bow at the mention of His name and obey His command, "Leave that person at once!" So what name are you going to glorify? Cancer? Are you going to magnify Lyme disease? Will you continue to praise the mighty power of diabetes in your life? Or will you humble yourself, bow your knee, and declare that Jesus is Lord? Will you do as your Lord Jesus tells you to do?

What does He tell us to do? He tells us to remember all of His benefits, who pardons all iniquities, heals all disease, redeems our lives from destruction, crowns us with lovingkindness and tender mercies, satisfies our mouths with good things and renews our youth like the eagle's (see Psalm 103:1-5).

It is time for God's people to glorify the name of Jehovah Rapha, who heals all disease, gives sight to the blind, opens deaf ears, strengthens the weak, causes the paralytics to walk, and releases those afflicted with demons. Glorify the name that is above all names—Jesus.

Reminder about what You Say

Remember, it is important what you say concerning the person standing in faith for the manifestation of their healing. To say, "She is very sick." Or "I'm praying for your health issues," only strengthen the disease. A quick reminder about what to say, "She needs our support to stand in faith for the manifestation of her healing." Or, "I am praying for the manifestation of your healing." These are better word choices, and they help to quicken the manifestation of the healing, too.

Natural Help and Faith

A reader writes, "I am seventy-two and my husband is seventy-seven years of age, we are Christians, and he has been diagnosed with Alzheimer's. I want to believe for him for total healing, but he does not want to stand in agreement with me because he says there isn't anything wrong with him. He's in denial of this disease. How do I deal with natural help offered for this situation, and also stand on the promise of God for healing? It feels like double mindedness to me and can sometimes cause anxiety for me."

This is a common scenario that you will have to face when standing in faith for healing, whether the illness is called Alzheimer's or another disease. Here is my response to the reader's questions and comments.

Dear Reader,

Thank you for writing and sharing your concerns and questions. I believe many are facing similar situations and the answers will help them just as much as they will help you.

First of all, I am not sure from your letter if your husband is aware of this diagnosis or not, but I do know this much, you cannot go against the will of another person. But if this disease has progressed to the point that he is unaware of what is happening with his mind, then in the natural he cannot make a decision for himself. Therefore, you become the one making the decisions for him, because he is unable to think with a clear mind for himself.

Second, when it comes to matters of faith, your natural age has no influence over the situation. What does have the influence in this situation is whether or not you believe. As a believer in Jesus Christ, you have authority over all sickness and disease, and this includes Alzheimer's as well. And the faith elements and strategies that I have shared throughout this work are your spiritual weapons you will use to overcome this attack on your husband's mind.

Speaking of faith strategies, here is one for this situation for you to activate immediately.

1. Form a support team to help you in this endeavor of faith.
2. Fill the atmosphere of your home or hospital room with faith.
3. Speak aloud healing Scriptures.
4. Write a confession of faith for his healing and deliverance.
5. Daily pray according to the strategies of prayer that I have shared with you earlier in this work over him.
6. Pray in the Spirit over him.
7. Anoint his pillow and his favorite chair with a little oil.

8. Confess and act out faith for his healing.

9. Play worship music 24/7.

10. Play healing teachings in his room, or wherever he likes to sit.

11. Saturate your home with healing and faith.

And third, to answer your question about what to do when natural help is offered. As long as the natural help does not compromise your faith for healing, or your faith for healing is not misplaced because of this natural help, all is well, go ahead. But if your faith is placed in the natural help, then no, don't do it.

Here is an example of what I mean. Someone else dies from the same disease that you are working your faith to overcome this disease and to manifest the physical healing, but this other person has leftover medication and it is offered to you to try and use. You think it is a Godsend, or God's provision. Without realizing it, all your faith goes into the pills and not giving thought or reason to the fact that the other person with the same disease died from the disease. The pills did not do them any good. All your faith transfers from the redemptive blood of Jesus to human reasoning and human experiments to heal. The enemy is tricky, and we need to be well-discerning in every area of life in these situations.

We've discussed about building and forming a support group that works, now let's learn how to compose our own confession of faith for healing in the last chapter of this work.

CHAPTER 18

WRITE A CONFESSION OF FAITH FOR YOUR HEALING

I am a firm believer that faith needs to be proactive to make a difference. Jesus always told the people to put their faith into action, to do something after He ministered healing to them. As the Word says, *"Faith by itself, if it does not have works, is dead"* (James 2:17).

One of my readers, Karen, and her husband, have been believing for the healing of their son from numerous ailments. One desired healing was to be healed from daily seizures. He was suffering from many seizures every day. Let's look at some of the steps of faith they have put into practice.

1. They are Christians.

2. They believe in the healing power of the Holy Spirit.

3. They have been praying and fasting as a family.

4. Members in the church they attend have been praying for their son.

5. They have asked the elders to anoint him with oil and to pray for him.

They still were not seeing the desired changes. I suggested to Karen that she write a confession of faith for healing and start to declare this over her son. She took to heart what I had been teaching her and wrote a confession of faith for her son's healing. After the first reading of this confession, the daily seizures stopped.

Karen's Praise Report

Be blessed and encouraged as you read Karen's praise report.

> I finally got this [confession of faith] written up this past weekend, and my husband and I pray it over our son every night before he goes to bed, and I pray it every morning with him (he loves to cuddle up with me while I have my morning time with God, so I just read the Scriptures out loud to him).
>
> I gave a copy to our prayer minister and also a copy to our son's children's church director, who is a great woman of faith. She prayed it over him in children's church on Sunday.
>
> The first part of the healing confession is Scriptures of healing and authority that we claim, and the second part is detailed commands for specific spirits that need to leave and areas of his body that need healing.
>
> Since we began praying and claiming this confession on Sunday night, he has not had any seizures, and we also are seeing the depression lifting off of him. Praise God! A few days later I received another praise report from Karen: "Our son is continuing to prosper in all areas—he has his energy back, he is achieving tasks at school that they've been trying to teach him all year, he is giggling and smiling again, and he is starting to say words again, and he has his appetite back."

I am so blessed by this family and that they choose to put their faith in action for their son—that they are teachable and willing to work the Word of God. Are you?

It's Your Turn

Throughout this entire work I have been teaching you about the prophetic and healing power of the spoken word and now I encourage you to write a confession of faith for your healing and to speak it over yourself and / or your loved one(s) daily. I have given to you many examples of this in Chapter 8, Prayer Strategies: Verbal Elements of Faith to Heal.

Don't allow the intimidation of the enemy to set in. With the foundational power of your words, you are going to emulate Jesus, hold your tongue, refrain from speaking out negative and poisonous word curses, and activate the creative and positive blessing of your words. Remember, you have the power of life and death in your tongue.

Now it is time to take these biblical truths and put them into action. Let's start this process and write our confession of faith for healing. How do we do this?

With a little investigation, we can find basic information about the disease and how it attacks the physical body. We need to remember that our purpose for this brief time of study is not so we become fearful and surrender to its wickedness. But that we become aware of its tactics and come up with a strategic battle plan against it.

After we have done a brief study of its pathology and what it seeks to destroy, then it is time to brainstorm and write a faith confession for healing. When we write this confession, we need to combat the sickness and the symptoms with prophetic and healing words of faith that will release life and healing.

This confession of faith is a base tool that you will use to create the atmosphere of faith necessary for healing to manifest. These words of faith will help to bolster your own faith in the power of the spoken word that God has set in motion for all people, including you.

To get started, ask yourself a few questions:

1. Who is this confession of faith for healing for?

2. What battle is this person facing?

3. Is there a demon spirit involved, such as a spirit of death or a spirit of fear?

4. What is this disease attacking?

5. What are the physical symptoms of this illness?

6. What needs to happen in the physical realm for this manifestation of healing?

7. You will be doing this in the name of the Lord; which name of Jesus will you access? (See Chapter 7, Sharpen Your Spiritual Use of Words: Access the Different Powers of His Names.)

Okay, you've done your short investigation of this disease. You've written down the pathology of this disease, now you will combat the negative with the positive pathology to healing through Jesus.

For example, a man writes that he is fighting against ALS, and it appears in the natural realm that it is overtaking his life. He needs a confession of faith for healing from this wretched disease that is attacking the nerve cells in his brain and spinal cord and is destroying his voluntary muscles, which is stealing the voluntary movement in his arms, legs, speech, and the ability to swallow and breathe freely.

Here is the written confession of faith for his healing:

> In the name of Jehovah Rapha, the Lord who heals (name of person), we use the keys of the Kingdom of Heaven that we have been given and we bind, lock up, and evict the spirit of death, via ALS, that is attacking your body. With these same keys we loose, we release the power of the Holy Spirit into your body. We decree that you will live and not waste away and die. We speak life and regeneration into your nerve cells in your brain and spinal cord, and into your voluntary muscles. We release creative miracles into your muscles, and say that they are nourished supernaturally, and that all scarring and hardening dissolve. Motor neurons regenerate

and send impulses to the muscle fibers and normal muscle movement return. Muscles be strengthened, and life return to the arms and legs, and speech, swallowing, and breathing be normal again. We declare all of this in Jesus' mighty name, amen.

Apply Spiritual Multiplication to the Power of Words

Increase the healing power of the tongue and make copies of your confession of faith for healing and give it to people who want to pray in faith for you. Ask them if they will commit to pray this aloud several times a day for you. I love the healing power of the Holy Spirit. Not only does the power heal the physical body, but the life of the person is forever changed. As is the case with one of my regular readers of my daily devotional sent via email.

Other Ways to Spiritually Multiply the Power of Your Words

- Record your healing confession of faith on your phone and play it several times a day to keep yourself uplifted in your faith for your healing.

- Record it on a CD and play it quietly 24/7. In doing so, you exercise godly wisdom and allow the power of the spoken word to work on your behalf.

- Activate the power of the healing Scriptures by reading them aloud. (I offer 100 faith and healing Scriptures for you for free on my website in a pdf format at http://author-beckydvorak.com/wp-content/uploads/2018/03/100-faith-and-healing-scriptures.pdf).

- Gather believers and pray in agreement using your written confession of faith for healing.

- Ask these believers to pray in the Spirit for your healing.

The point in all of this is to activate the prophetic and healing power of words, remember there is the power of life and death in our words. Activate their power on behalf of the person in need, whether that's you or someone else you love.

In Conclusion

In conclusion, we've researched what the Bible has to say to us concerning the power of our spoken words—and tapped into the flow of their healing power. We've honed in on the message of Proverbs 18:21, that our words have the power of life and death in them—and also realize that every word counts. What we say does make a difference. If we continue to speak symptoms, sickness, disease, and death, those negative words will take root within our spirits and grow—and eventually produce death in our physical bodies.

But we choose to be wise and sharpen our spiritual use of our words, activate prayer strategies and elements of faith to turn on the spigot of the Spirit, and speak life over our bodies by the power of prophetic healing. We prophesy to our bones, overcome premature death, recreate worn-out body parts, and set in motion strength and healing through the power of our tongue.

APPENDIX

ANSWERS TO CHAPTER QUESTIONS

Answers for Chapter 1—Emulate the Living Word

1. The prophetic power of healing is on her tongue.

2. The effectiveness of the prophetic.

3. The power of His faith-filled words.

4. Holy Spirit.

5. Childlike faith.

6. Jesus at His word.

7. Jesus gave His consenting spoken words, *"Nevertheless not My will, but Yours, be done."*

8. Ask God to forgive you, write the negative phrase down in a notebook and ask Him to teach you how to restate that comment so that it produces godly results in your physical body or situation.

Answers for Chapter 2—Hold Your Tongue

1. Prophesy life or death.

2. Control your words and speak according to God's healing covenant.

3.   A bountiful harvest in life.

4.   Unnecessary havoc and stress.

5.   The epidemic disease of "me, myself, and I." The power of words. He lies.

6.   The devil is a mastermind at trickery with words. He is always looking for a way to make God's people fall.

7.   You first must handle the truth.

8.   Your physical body will follow after the direction of your unhealthy words and will spiral downward into sickness and disease.

9.   Your life.

Answers for Chapter 3—Negative and Poisonous Word Curses

1.   Curses are unfavorable utterances verbalized to ravage destruction upon another person.

2.   Use the power of the spoken word and declare, "I have a blood covenant with the Father, and every curse has been broken, including this one. And in Jesus' name, your evil works have no effect on me."

3.   The name of our Lord Jesus, Yeshua.

4.   Deliverance and transformation in the Word of God.

5.   The answer lies in the power of the spoken words, and in this case with the parents it's the lack of them. And so the enemy takes advantage of the parents not speaking up and uses all of these means of warped entertainment to enslave their listeners and readers to the evil power of their message.

6.   According to the Word, faith operates by love, and love alone.

7.   Because ministering angels are hindered and destructive powers of demons are released.

8. They produce.

9. The poisonous tongue.

Answers for Chapter 4—The Creative and Positive Blessing of Words

1. The direction of your life.

2. It declares praises to Jehovah Rapha and His faithfulness to keep His healing promises. It produces supernatural healing with the power of prophetic words. It encourages trust to believe for God's miraculous ways. It denies ownership of sickness and disease by claiming the power of the blood. It protects the body from sickness and disease by prohibiting its entrance.

3. Healing properties.

4. Edification. To build up.

5. He activates the power of the name of the Lord, and then he boldly prophesies what is about to take place. And he confidently can speak forth such bold prophetic utterance because he knows the battle belongs to his God.

6. God's grace, goodness, and favor toward humans.

7. A weak spot.

8. No.

9. You must be born again, baptized in the Holy Spirit, transformation by the power of God's Word, live the Word, repent when you say things that are mean or hurtful.

10. *Creative.*

Answers for Chapter 5—The Power of Life and Death in the Tongue

1. The words that we speak.

2. The supernatural *dunamus,* dynamite and explosive power of the Spirit.

3. To release healing, to create miracles, and to build one another up in the faith, not to tear down and discourage one another.

4. By the power of your spoken words.

5. Develop the healthy habit of daily Bible study, ponder the message of the Scriptures you are studying throughout the day, verbalize these verses out loud repeatedly, and live out the Word, do what it says.

6. Faith.

7. So that the demonic power behind it clearly understands you will not tolerate this sickness or physical problem anymore.

8. Symptoms.

Answers for Chapter 6—Does My Tongue Need Healing?

1. Radical healing.

2. A positive response of faith.

3. To make a difference, not to blend in or to be controlled by it.

4. To recognize and admit that you need this healing in the first place.

5. They will reap a heap of garbage in every area of your life.

6. *That both he and those he is called to prophesy to are defiled in their speech.*

7. *We need to repent from a negative form of vocabulary that goes against the promises of God so our words can be sanctified and we can prophesy healing, health, and the miraculous as the Spirit wills.*

Answers for Chapter 7—Wield Your Sword of the Spirit

1. A spiritual battle against demonic forces.

2. With the supernatural weaponry that God has equipped His people with.

3. God gives us a supernatural weapon called the Sword of the Spirit, His Holy Word.

4. The Word of God.

5. Dangerous and ineffective.

6. You cannot destroy the works of satan.

7. By sharpening them upon the honing stone, the all-powerful Holy Scriptures.

8. With another mature believer, train and challenge, rebuke and edify one another with the Scriptures.

9. To start, open your Bible, read and study it, and do what it says to do. To keep the edge of your blade sharp, you need to be consistent, faithful, and spend time in the Word alone with God, and sharpen your skills with others.

Answers for Chapter 8—Prayer Strategies

1. Fellowship between you and God.

2. *Palal*, and it means to intervene and interpose (intercede).

3. If it is a private and sensitive matter, then it should be prayed for privately, or in a group of two or three very trustworthy and mature individuals as a prayer of agreement.

4. The Greek word is *deēsis;* it means "a request or petition." The biblical usage of this word is seeking, asking, and entreating from God or from man.

5. It is a personal prayer request for yourself.

6. Others.

7. Faith is a substance, a supernatural foundation.

8. Your relationship and communication with Elohim, the Father, Son, and Holy Spirit.

9. It is prayer mixed with faith.

10. The Hebrew word is *yeda*. It means to give thanks. Jubilee.

11. The Hebrew word is *sebó;* it means to personally esteem; to hold something (someone) in high respect; showing the reverence or awe (veneration) of someone who is devout. And the physical position of the body is not that of jubilant dance, but often in a humble position down on our knees or prostrate before Him.

12. It centers on the person of God, who He is, rather than what He does or has done for us.

13. *"If two of you agree on earth concerning anything that they ask, it will be done for them by My Father in heaven. For where two or three are gathered together in My name, I am there in the midst of them."*

14. The keys of the Kingdom of Heaven.

15. The power to open and shut.

16. The Greek word is *basileia. It means royal power, kingship, dominion, and rule.*

17. *Whatever you bind on earth will be bound in heaven, and whatever you loose on earth will be loosed in heaven.*

18. The Greek word is *deo;* it means to tie, fasten with chains, or to throw into chains, to forbid, or prohibit something.

19. The Greek word is *lyo;* it means to loose any person or thing that is tied or fastened to someone or something.

Answers for Chapter 9—Deliverance Strategies from Various Spirits

1. Demon possession and oppression.

2. The spoken Word of God. The strategies will be different and much more intense according to the direction of the Spirit.

Answers for Chapter 10—Confessions of Faith for Healing

1. The Greek word for confession is *homologeó* and it means to speak the same thing, or to agree.

2. The manifestation of your healing comes to pass.

Answers for Chapter 11—Declaration of Faith

1. You make an official verbal statement about something you already have or possess.

2. It encourages your faith and reminds you of your spiritual blessings.

Answers for Chapter 12—Decrees of Faith

1. *Gazar;* it means to cut, to divide, or to separate.

2. The Word of God. They produce in the physical realm what they are verbally sent out to do.

Answers for Chapter 13—The Power of Your Supernatural Language

1. We will speak with new tongues.

2. We edify ourselves.

3. The recreated spirit.

4. In our weaknesses.

5. He makes intercession for us with groanings, which cannot be uttered.

6. Pray that we may interpret.

7. God.

8. Mysteries.

9. Forbid to speak in tongues in public.

10. Praying always with all prayer and supplication in the Spirit.

11. All the saints.

12. Build yourself up in the most holy faith.

Answers for Chapter 14—Word of Knowledge

1. The supernatural ability to know facts about a situation that are happening in the present tense, there is no future telling in the word of knowledge. You would not otherwise have knowledge of the situation, but for the spiritual insight of the Holy Spirit.

2. First Corinthians 12:8.

3. To minister into the lives of people.

4. To know that God hears and cares for their needs.

5. It's a sign that Jesus Christ is real, and it opens their hearts to receive the message God has prepared for them.

6. It gives detailed direction about how the Lord would have them minister.

Answers for Chapter 15—Call Things into Being

1. When He cried out from the cross, "It is finished."

2. Healed us.

3. By His stripes.

4. *Dunamus* power.

5. The power of your words.

6. You are to *deactivate* the deadly acts of satan against your body and *activate* Jehovah Rapha's life-giving power and create or recreate what you have need of for yourself.

ABOUT THE AUTHOR

Becky Dvorak is a prophetic healing evangelist, and author about faith for the miraculous. She is a firm believer in the healing power of Jesus Christ and travels worldwide to equip churches and leaders to walk in the supernatural power of the Holy Spirit with signs and wonders following. She also leads short-term mission groups.

She and her husband, David, are founders and overseers of Healing and Miracles International with a mission of empowering people to heal, establish worldwide healing and rescue centers, evangelize the nations, and exalt Jesus Christ.

She is also cofounder and overseer of Fundaccion VIDA Ilimitada and LIFE Tender Mercy Home in Guatemala for children who have been orphaned, abandoned, or born infected with the HIV virus but are in the healing process.

She and David have been married for almost 40 years and have resided in Guatemala, Central America, as missionaries since 1994. She is the mother of three biological and five adopted children. She has one son-in-law, two daughters-in-law, and is the grandmother of ten.

Please visit her website for more information about her ministry and involvement opportunities: http://authorbeckydvorak.com/.